MODERN
NATIONS
—OF THE—
WORLD

CHINA

TITLES IN THE MODERN NATIONS OF THE WORLD SERIES INCLUDE:

Canada
China
Cuba
England
Germany
Italy
Mexico
Russia
South Korea

MODERN
NATIONS
—OF THE—
WORLD

CHINA

BY ROBERT GREEN

LUCENT BOOKS
P.O. BOX 289011
SAN DIEGO, CA 92198-9011

Library of Congress Cataloging-in-Publication Data

Green, Robert, 1969–
    China / Robert Green.
        p.   cm. — (Modern nations of the world)
    Includes bibliographical references and index.
    Summary: Discusses the history, geography, culture, and current
conditions in the People's Republic of China.
    ISBN 1-56006-440-4 (alk. paper)
    1. China—Juvenile literature.   2. China—History—20th century—
Juvenile literature.   [1. China.]   I. Title.   II. Series.
DS706.G745   1999
951—dc21   98-30578
                                                                                    CIP
                                                                                    AC

Copyright © 1999 by Lucent Books, Inc.
P.O. Box 289011, San Diego, CA 92198-9011
Printed in the U.S.A.

CONTENTS

INTRODUCTION

THE MIDDLE KINGDOM

China is as large as it is populous. Of the nations of the world, it ranks third in size—only Russia and Canada are larger. It is a giant land mass occupying the greater part of eastern Asia and lying at about the same distance between the North Pole and the equator as the United States does.

China's geography played a central role in the development of its antique civilization. For most of its history China was cut off from other civilizations by the Pacific Ocean to the east, the barren steppes of central Asia to the west, and the mighty Himalaya Mountains to the southwest. The result was that China developed in relative isolation.

Contact with foreigners, both in trade and in war, was limited primarily to nomadic tribes. The goods and ideas of ancient China reached the outside world through a series of trade routes known as the Silk Road, which connected China with markets to the west. The ancient Chinese traders who saw their wares teeter away on nomadic caravans believed that China and its civilization were indeed the middle of the world. Although the official name of the country today is the People's Republic of China, the Chinese commonly refer to their country as Zhong Guo (the Middle Kingdom).

THE GENIUS THAT WAS CHINA

The Chinese certainly have reason to be proud of their civilization. Their recorded history dates back nearly three thousand years. As early as the sixteenth century B.C., Chinese emperors received the "mandate of heaven," took their place on the peacock throne, and established the earliest-known dynasty.

The genius of the Chinese empire was administrative. A good emperor was one who improved the lives of the common people by such practical things as tax reform and improvements to waterways. The role of government in a country so vast and so diverse cannot be underestimated.

Even China's most celebrated philosopher, Confucius, was concerned primarily with a model social organization and the ethics of good government.

Under the dynastic system, the emperor and his administrators, known as mandarins for the language they spoke, brought a stability to China that allowed remarkable innovation. Paper, porcelain (often called china), gunpowder, the compass, the clock, and movable type are all Chinese inventions. No less impressive than China's material creations are China's intellectual achievements in philosophy, history, literature, and the visual arts.

A WAKING GIANT

The Chinese empire dominated Asia for two thousand years. Neighbors, such as Korea and Vietnam, were vassal states. Only with the arrival of great numbers of European powers in the late eighteenth century was China laid low. By 1911 the erosion was complete, and the world's longest-lived political structure collapsed. More than a century of humiliation at the hands of Western powers was put to an end only in 1949 with the proclamation of the founding of China's first communist government, the People's Republic of China.

Chief among China's historical accomplishments are its works of architecture, including ornately styled bridges, temples, and pagodas.

Today China is a modern nation, but the legacy of China's ancient supremacy in Asia is still visible. The Chinese communities in Singapore, Malaysia, and Indonesia are vibrant, wealthy, and influential, and Taiwan and Hong Kong are considered two of the booming "tiger economies" of Asia.

China is struggling to modernize. The economy, moving away from its communist roots, is undergoing a dizzying boom. With the new prosperity and openness has come a period of excitement not felt since the founding of the People's Republic. China is once again on the verge of greatness, once again poised to take its traditional role as the great power of Asia. Its potential lies in the riches of its land and in its vibrant and swollen population—it is the most populous nation on earth, housing one-fifth of humanity. "China?" Napoleon once remarked. "There lies a sleeping giant. Let him sleep! For when he wakes he will move the world."[1]

THE LAND

To understand China's history, its language, and the characteristics of the Chinese people, nothing could be so important as a grasp of China's geography. China is a giant land mass, occupying most of the habitable land of eastern Asia and a great deal of land that is scarcely populated.

China is a country of remarkably varied climates and landscapes, much like the United States. In fact, China and the United States are not so different in shape and are nearly equal in size, with China being slightly larger. The two countries also lie roughly between the same latitudes; the continental United States is bordered by the latitudes of about 49 degrees to the north and 25 degrees to the south, while China extends a little more to the north (54 degrees) and considerably more to the south (18 degrees). The distance from northern Maine to the southern tip of Florida is about the same as the east coast of China, from the province of Liaoning to the island of Hainan. China extends farther north, and so has a longer north-south distance than that of the United States, but the east-west measurements are more nearly equal.

If one were to drive along the coast, from southeastern China northward into Manchuria, the northernmost part of China, one would encounter many climate variations. Generally, the more northward one travels in China the more the temperature cools. The southernmost part of China has a tropical climate, and just north of that a broad expanse of land has semitropical conditions. Here, average temperatures in the summer range between 77°F (25°C) and 86°F (30°C), not so different from northern China. Winter temperatures, however, are much warmer than in the north; in the south, temperatures do not fall below 14°F (-10°C), and the average is just above the freezing point. Frosts occur only occasionally, and in the southernmost tropical areas not at all.

Northern China, which also experiences hot, humid summers, has an average nighttime temperature below the freezing point from October to April. In southern Manchuria the average temperature in January is 16°F (-9°C), while in

The Yangtze is one of the "ten thousand rivers" that traverse the Chinese landscape.

the central Manchurian city of Harbin, the average temperature in January is -4°F (-20°C). Still farther north, where Manchuria borders Siberia, permafrost is common.

WESTERN CHINA

Mao Zedong, China's first communist leader, described China as having "ten thousand rivers, a thousand mountains."[2] Mountains and high plateaus cover one-third of China, giving rise to one common description of China as the "Land of Mountains."

One way to imagine China's topography is as a giant slope, dropping steadily from the west eastward toward the sea. This slope can be divided into three declining steps: western China, central China, and eastern China. The Qinghai-Tibet Plateau occupies the greater part of Xizang (Tibet) and Qinghai Provinces, which cover most of southwestern China, and is the most extensive plateau in the world. It lies at an average height of more than 13,200 feet above sea level, and is sometimes referred to as the "rooftop of the world." Mountain ranges sprout out of the plateau at frequent intervals. The largest ranges are the Kunlun, Altun, and Qilian, which have peaks that reach a soaring 23,100 feet. To the south near the border of Nepal, the Qinghai-Tibet Plateau rises into the Himalayan mountain range, the site of the world's highest mountains.

The plateau's height and remoteness from the sea cause severe temperatures, averaging in some areas below the freezing point and in others around 45°F (7°C). Rainfall is sparse, but a number of rivers wind down the mountain passes. Much of the water, however, is collected in upland basins forming landlocked lakes. Qinghai Lake is located in this region, and with a surface area of 1,600 square miles, it is China's largest lake (though a shallow lake called Lop Nor in Xinjiang expands and shrinks drastically and can reach up to 2,650 square miles).

To the north of the Qinghai-Tibet Plateau lies Xinjiang Province. With an area of 637,000 square miles, Xinjiang is China's largest province and covers one-sixth of China's total area. In Xinjiang, the Qinghai-Tibet Plateau slopes downward from the Kunlun Shan mountain range into the Takla Makan Desert. In fact, more than one-fifth of Xinjiang is desert. This is a cold, arid region with an annual rainfall of less than ten inches. It is very different from the common image of China as a land of lush green rice paddies.

Xinjiang alternates between mountains and depressions. Aside from the Takla Makan Desert, the lowlands include the Junggar Basin in the north and the Tarim Basin, which encloses the Takla Makan Desert. These two depressions are separated by the Tian Shan mountain chain, and to the west the Pamirs separate China from Pakistan, India, Afghanistan,

Much of western China is dominated by large mountains and high-altitude plateaus.

Tajikistan, and Kyrgyzstan. The shifts in elevation can be quite dramatic; peaks in the Tian Shan reach as high as 17,000 feet, while the Turpan Valley lies 505 feet below sea level, making it the second-lowest place on earth. The longest river in Xinjiang is the Tarim River, which empties into its largest lake, Lop Nor. At the northernmost part of the province, where China borders Kazakhstan and Mongolia, the Altai Mountains form part of the Mongolian Altai range.

CENTRAL CHINA

The Qinghai-Tibet Plateau slopes gently downward into the Yunnan-Guizhou Plateau of the southern part of central China, the second of the three steps toward the sea. The mountain ranges of western Sichuan and Yunnan Provinces are still quite high; the highest peak, the Gongga Shan in Sichuan, is 24,900 feet high. But as the ranges slope into the Yunnan-Guizhou Plateau, altitudes level to somewhere between 6,000 and 9,000 feet above sea level. The plateau

THE ISLAND OF HAINAN

Hainan, located in the South China Sea thirty miles off the coast of Guangdong Province, is China's largest island (excluding Taiwan). It has a long history of association with China; as early as the seventh century A.D., imperial officials were exiled to Hainan for their offenses. Despite the presence of the Chinese, Hainan's original inhabitants, the Li, were dominant until the fifteenth century, when a steady stream of Chinese immigrants forced them into the hills.

One of the prinicipal immigrant groups to Hainan was the clannish Hakka—northern Chinese who had immigrated to southern China. Hakka clans developed closed trading communities and greatly increased Hainan's role in maritime trade. The most unwelcome immigrants were the Japanese, who occupied the island in 1939.

In 1988, the Chinese government granted Hainan provincial status—it had previously been part of Guangdong Province—and declared the island a Special Economic Zone. Since then, Hainan's economy has boomed. Tourists flock to the palm-lined white-sand beaches, and tropical fruits grow in abundance. Other major industries include rubber production, iron-ore and coal mining, and fishing.

CHINA'S PROVINCES

covers most of the two provinces for which it is named. Yunnan has, perhaps, the most marvelous weather in China. Although the landscape varies greatly between mountains and valleys, the climate is temperate and usually sunny. Temperatures average between 68°F (20°C) and 77°F (25°C) in July and between 41°F (5°C) and 50°F (10°C) in January. The hills are heavily forested, yet there are many upland areas for grazing animals, and the valleys receive regular rainfall, making the land fertile.

The Sichuan Basin lies between the Yunnan-Guizhou Plateau and the plateau of Gansu, Shaanxi, and Shanxi Provinces to the north of Yunnan and Guizhou. The Sichuan Basin is also known as the Red Basin for its concentration of red sandstone. It is one of the most fertile and most populous regions in China. The hilly countryside is covered with rich soil, and the monsoon climate ensures mild winters and long warm summers. The variety of crops grown there have made the regional food of Sichuan famous the world over. To the north of the Sichuan Basin lie the Qinling mountain range and the plateau of Gansu, Shaanxi, and Shanxi. This is still fairly mountainous land, but the altitude is lower than to the south or the west and averages between 3,000 and 6,000 feet. Still farther to the north rises another of China's uplands, the Mongolian Plateau. The altitude is fairly low, averaging around 6,000 feet, and the rolling landscape has provided pastureland for the raising of camels (to the west) and goats, sheep, cattle, and horses (to the east) for centuries. There is a large sweep of arid land known as the Gobi Desert. Annual rainfall on the western side of the plateau is less than ten inches, but increases gradually toward the eastern side.

EASTERN CHINA

The final step in the slow eastward descent of the Chinese landscape consists of the plains and low mountains of eastern China. This is the part of China that the world knows best, with its vast floodplains and low-lying rice paddies. This is the home of most of China's 1.2 billion people. The many small provinces provide a quick visual clue that this was the origin of Chinese civilization, much as the small states on the eastern seaboard of the United States developed before the vast, mountainous western states.

Eastern China is home to many of the nation's rice paddies as well as the majority of China's 1.2 billion people.

THE PARADISE OF GUILIN

Nestled in the countryside of Guangxi Province in southern China lies the town of Guilin (which means "forest of cinnamon trees"). The town is famed for its encircling hills, which display some of the strangest rock formations on the planet. The unnatural appearance of the hills is a testament to their age. Over a span of some 200 million years, the peaks evolved into their present shapes.

The hills are formed from chalk (limestone) in what is known as a karstic formation. Wind and water eroded these soft hills into their fantastic shapes and burrowed out a number of equally fantastic caves. The names alone of the hills testify to their enchantment: the Mount of Unique Beauty, Whirlpool Hill, Mountain of Piled Brocades, Camel Hill, and Elephant Trunk Hill. The caves, such as Seven Star Cave, Dragon Refuge Cave, and the Cave of Returned Pearls, have spawned their own folklore, and many are inscribed with poems and Buddhist scripture.

Guilin has been, at various times, the home of the Ming court fleeing from the conquering Manchurians (founders of the Qing dynasty) and of writers, musicians, and artists fleeing the invading Japanese during World War II. In autumn the scent of cinnamon trees still fills the air, and with its many sparkling streams and celebrated hills, it is one of China's principal tourist attractions.

Eastern China can be divided into two distinct geographic and climatic zones: north and south. The division is marked from the point where China's bulging coastline reaches farthest into the East China Sea, near the famous trading port of Shanghai. From this point, the coastline slopes inward both to the north and to the south.

This geographic feature explains the differences between the climate of northeastern and southeastern China. During the summer months when the monsoon season determines the climate of much of eastern Asia, the winds blow in a northwesterly direction from the seas in the southeast. When the monsoon winds hit the coast in the south, they deposit rain. In the north, however, the winds blow right past the great bulge, and rain clouds are rarely carried inward to water the plains of northern China.

Northern China is therefore a good deal drier than southern China, and the color of its land tends more toward browns and yellows. This northern part of China, in fact, is called "Yellow China," because of the ochre-colored soil. The soil is yellow not just from the lack of rain, but also from the accumulation of loess, a fine wind-blown soil originating in the west, in the provinces of Gansu, Shaanxi, and Shanxi.

THE YELLOW RIVER

Loess is blown eastward throughout most of the year, coloring mountains, plains, and rivers with a yellowish hue. The principal river of northern China is the Yellow River (Huang He in Chinese), which gets its name from its loess-colored waters. The Yellow River follows the topographic descent from west to east. It originates in the Qinghai-Tibet Plateau and slithers through central China, north into Inner Mongolia, and finally onto the plains of northeastern China. After a total journey of 3,020 miles, making it the seventh-longest river in the world, it empties into the Yellow Sea, which is also named for its loess-colored waters.

The unpredictable flow of the Yellow River has long determined the way of life in northern China. Because of the low rainfall in the north, Chinese farmers have always diverted the waters of the Yellow River to irrigate their crops. Wheat, corn, sweet potatoes, watermelons, and peanuts are all watered in this way. Often the waters of the Yellow River run dry, and famine results. The Yellow River also floods frequently, causing the destruction of crops and villages.

THE YANGTZE RIVER

Just as the floodplains of northern China are watered by the Yellow River, the floodplains of southern China are watered by another great river, the Yangtze (or Chang Jiang, "Long River," in Chinese). Its proportions are even greater than those of the Yellow River. This west-to-east watercourse also originates high in the Qinghai-Tibet Plateau and travels over 3,720 miles before emptying into the East China Sea. It is the third-longest river in the world—only the Nile and the Amazon are longer—and it irrigates one-fifth of China.

A much greater quantity of water flows down the Yangtze: It pours some 7.5 million gallons per second into the East China Sea. The waters also flow more regularly; droughts and floods are far less common. When it does overrun its banks, however, the results can be devastating. In July 1998 heavy rains caused the worst Yangtze flood in forty-four years, killing over twelve hundred people and driving millions more from their homes. The Yangtze is navigable by steamer for several hundred miles upstream, making it an important transportation route.

The Yellow River winds through the city of Lanzhou in Gansu Province. The yellowish soil loess, which gives the Yellow River its name, originates in this area.

For thousands of years, rivers have provided transportation for the Chinese, who also added an extensive system of canals in early times. The most famous of the canals is the Grand Canal, stretching from the Yangtze northward to the Huai River in central China and farther north to the Yellow River and on to Beijing. The Grand Canal was strung together out of many older canals and was completed in the late 1280s during the reign of Kublai Khan. The Grand Canal was used from that time until 1855 when the Yellow River overran its banks and never returned to its original course, leaving much of the northern part of the canal dry.

AGRICULTURE

The waters of the Yangtze are largely free of the ochre silt of the Yellow River, and its clearer waters have earned it the name "Blue River." Loess is also noticeably absent from the surrounding countryside, and the land is a good deal greener than in the north. The south also receives the full generosity of the monsoon rains from spring to summer. The abundance of rain and the warm subtropical climate make this area the breadbasket of China. Rice is the principal crop. Two or three harvests can be reaped in one season.

Northern China was probably never heavily wooded, but ancient forests grew in the south. Farmers have since deforested most of the region for the rice paddies, and dense forests now exist only in the southwestern part of this region.

South of the Yangtze, hills and low mountain ranges rise more frequently than in the north. On the southern end of the Chinese coast, there exists one more great riverbed. This is the Pearl River (Zhu Jiang) Delta, where the North (Beijiang), West (Xijiang), and East (Dongjiang) Rivers spill into the South China Sea. The city of Canton (Guangzhou), one of China's busiest trading ports and an important manufacturing city, is located on the Pearl River Delta. Across the bay lies the island of Hong Kong, a former British colony that reverted to Chinese rule in 1997.

MANCHURIA

Northeast of the loess plains of "Yellow China" lie the three provinces of the region called Manchuria: Heilongjiang, Jilin, and Liaoning. Lowlands stretching from the Yellow Sea northward toward Russian Siberia comprise most of Manchuria.

China's rivers, including the Yangtze (pictured), have traditionally served as transportation and trading routes.

The lowlands are ringed by mountains: The Changbai Mountains and the Yalu River form a border with North Korea, the Greater Hinggan Mountains separate Manchuria from Inner Mongolia, and the Lesser Hinggan Mountains and the Amur River (Heilong Jiang) form a border with Russia.

Cultivation is possible in this extremely cold region. Winter wheat, sugar beets, corn, soybeans, and some other crops with short growing seasons are raised. But the importance of Manchuria lies in its mineral resources and dense forests. Since the discovery of oil fields, coal deposits, and several other mineral resources, Manchuria has at one time or other been fought over by the Chinese, Russians, and Japanese. The Japanese during their occupation from 1931 to 1945 exploited Manchuria's riches and introduced heavy industry.

Today it is the site of many of China's huge state-run factories. The Chinese are in the process of privatizing many of these industries. Unemployment has risen drastically in Manchuria's industrial cities, and the fate of workers in this area has always been a good indicator of changes in the Chinese economy.

THE LAND AND THE FUTURE

China's geography will undoubtedly play an important role in the nation's future. As the Chinese economy becomes more and more modern, the need for new energy sources increases. Resources in Xinjiang Province and other areas are just now being explored. The need for energy is the driving force behind the construction of the huge Three Gorges Dam

---

HONG KONG

The island of Hong Kong is situated about ninety miles southeast off the coast of the province of Guangdong (Canton) in the Pearl River estuary. This small island is famed for its green hills and natural harbors. Victoria Harbor was originally called Hong Kong ("fragrant harbor") in Chinese, giving the island its name.

Located just south of the Tropic of Cancer, Hong Kong shares the semitropical monsoon climate of the southern Chinese coast. Summer temperatures average between 77°F (25°C) and 88°F (31°C), and winter temperatures between 50°F (10°C) and 68°F (20°C). Humidity is oppressive in the summer and can hover around 90 percent. Its geography is rugged and mountainous; the island's highest point, Victoria Peak, rises to 1,818 feet and overlooks Victoria Harbor.

In 1842 as a result of the First Opium War, the island was awarded to the British. In the Second Opium War (1856–1858), the British expanded their prize to include the New Territories on the mainland across the water from Hong Kong, as well as Lantau Island (about twice the size of Hong Kong) and numerous other nearby islands. This collection of British-ruled territories is called simply Hong Kong. Under British rule, Hong Kong became one of the busiest trading centers in Asia. The British returned the colony to Chinese rule on July 1, 1997. It is now one of the most prosperous parts of the People's Republic of China.

now being built on the Yangtze River. This project alone could radically alter China's topography by submerging thousands of miles of land under water, creating new lakes, and displacing entire villages. The ambitious size of this project resembles the ancient imperial building projects, such as the Great Wall and the Grand Canal.

China's most pressing problem today is overpopulation. But the Chinese are fortunate; they might need look no further than their rich, vast lands to ease the pressures of overpopulation.

The view of Hong Kong from Victoria Peak reveals a thriving, modern metropolis. After more than 150 years of British rule, this economic hub has been returned to Chinese rule.

THE EXPANSION OF THE CHINESE POPULATION

One of the greatest obstacles to understanding China has always been the difficulty of defining exactly who the Chinese are. Westerners have vivid pictures of old Chinese types: silk-robed court officials, teetering women with bound feet, and revolutionary Chinese clad in blue "Mao suits." But these types have vanished.

Today, the urban populace of the People's Republic of China certainly appears more like people from other modern countries. Most Chinese wear Western-style clothes, and modern conveniences such as television, movies, and cellular phones are increasingly common. But 80 percent of China's population still lives in the countryside. Although life in the countryside is also changing, the life of a farmer today is still remarkably similar to that of a farmer two thousand years ago.

The contradiction here lies in the fact that although China has changed drastically in the past hundred years, many aspects of traditional Chinese civilization remain in its modern society. It is hard to generalize about a country that is so vast and so populous. Moreover, China is in the midst of rapid and fundamental changes today, and the younger generations are considerably different in their outlook and ambitions than their elders. So what can be said of the Chinese?

The most telling fact about this diverse population is that the vast majority identify themselves as Han Chinese. This identity comes not from living within China's borders, which have changed over time, or from a common spoken language, but from a strong cultural identity. The Han Chinese make up 93 percent of the population. Originally the Han were a mixture of several different groups of people. Their origins can be traced to early settlements on the eastern China floodplains. This region represents one of the most ancient sites of human development.

PREHISTORIC CHINA

Han Chinese fall into the racial grouping of the Mongoloid family of people, to which the majority of Asians belong. Their features include dark shiny hair, almond-shaped eyes, and a shorter stature than that of the average European. Remarkable finds at a cave complex called Zhoukoudian in northern China gave the world Peking Man (Beijing Man), an example of *Homo erectus* that lived about six hundred thousand years ago in the middle Pleistocene age. These early cave dwellers used crude stone tools and lived much like other Stone Age societies. Their features resembled those of the Indians of North America more than the modern Chinese.

Modern China retains elements of its ancient past while adopting Western technologies and products.

There is no proven link between the fossil remains of Peking Man and other specimens of *Homo erectus*. The first communities to resemble the modern Chinese in appearance also inhabited the floodplains of eastern China, primarily in the valleys of the Yellow, the Wei (a tributary of the Yellow), and the Yangtze Rivers. Sometime around nine thousand years ago, these early Chinese tamed animals and planted crops, allowing a more settled life. The land, with its fertile plains and navigable rivers, fostered these settlements.

Irrigation supplied by the various river systems offset the scarcity of rain and allowed the early Chinese to work the loess soils of northern China. Chinese farming communities set a pattern for a distinctly Chinese civilization to take shape. The fact that the Chinese did not pass through a long stage of hunting and gathering, but developed fixed communities early on, is remarkable in comparison with other civilizations. The farthest borders of settled life for the Chinese traditionally marked the limits of civilization. The nomads to the north and west of the river valleys were considered barbarians.

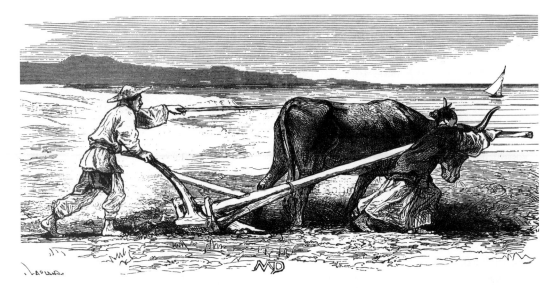

Due to the natural irrigation system created by rivers, the Chinese established farming communities early in the development of their society. These first communities developed and merged to form the Xia dynasty and initiated the dynastic system.

In these early settlements, the Chinese cultivated rice and millets, wove fabrics, hunted with bow and arrow, and produced decorated pottery. As the settlements grew, a complex hierarchy arose, defensive walls were erected around villages, metal was worked, and the rudiments of a written language were established. By the twenty-first century B.C., the settlements had coalesced into a kingdom known as the Xia dynasty about which few hard facts are known. Modern Chinese historians consider this the starting point of the dynastic system.

A marvelous discovery in the 1920s confirmed the existence of the next Chinese dynasty, the Shang (ca. 1600 B.C.), previously considered to be mythical. Digging near the ancient Shang capital of Anyang, archaeologists unearthed charred and cracked fragments of bone and turtle shells, collectively known as oracle bones, which were inscribed with questions and in some cases answers. The Shang, and probably the Xia before them, used these bones for divination. Questions were carved into the shoulder bone of an ox, sheep, or pig, or a turtle's shell, and then held to the fire. The heat caused the bone or shell to crack, and the answers to the questions were interpreted from the fissures.

The oracle bones reveal a preoccupation with questions of lineage, fertility, and fortune. The emperor and his nobles consulted the oracles most of all. Common among the inquiries were questions about the royal family and the wisdom of decisions concerning state matters. Shang religion was closely tied to the Shang state, and consultation with the gods was essential to government.

The early Chinese were animistic. Their gods dwelled in the rivers, forests, and the sky, and just about everyplace else. At the head of the various animistic gods was Shang Di, the high god of heaven. Winning Shang Di's favor was essential to govern, for Shang Di controlled all natural phenomena: Crops sprang in abundance when he was pleased, and rivers overran their beds, causing destruction and famine, when he was displeased.

The beliefs and rituals of early Chinese civilization set the pattern for Chinese religion for thousands of years and would later be modified by Confucius into the state religion of China.

CHINESE MYTHOLOGY

The rich body of Chinese mythology includes the story of Pan Gu, the first man. According to this legend:

> Before the heavens and the earth were opened, the universe was all in darkness, a mass of confusion in the shape of a great egg. And there, in that egg, was the one called Pan Gu. He had been sleeping and growing in that egg for eighteen thousand years.
>
> One day he opened his eyes and looked around and saw nothing but terrible darkness. He could hardly breathe! A rage began to grow within him. "Why am I, Pan Gu, in such darkness? Why am I in this egg?"
>
> He flung out his arms in anger and his hand touched a big axe; no one knows where it came from. He grabbed the axe and began to swing it wildly from side to side through the mass of confusion. Then suddenly, "Crash!" the sound of a thousand thunders echoed through the universe. The great egg cracked open!
>
> Slowly then, and quietly, all lightness rose up to form the heavens and all that was thick and heavy dropped down to form the earth.
>
> When Pan Gu saw this, he sighed deeply, and he thought, "What if heaven and earth close up again?"
>
> So he began to support the heavens with his head and hold down the earth under his feet. When he felt

the heavens and earth growing, he grew too. Each day the heavens grew one Zhang higher, and the earth one Zhang lower. So Pan Gu grew too each day. For eighteen thousand years he grew until the top of heaven was ninety thousand li away from earth. And there it was fixed. And there it stayed unchanging.

For all those eighteen thousand years Pan Gu tirelessly supported the heavens. When he saw that the heavens and earth were finally fixed, he breathed deeply one last time and wearily lay down to die. And as he was dying his body slowly began to shift, sinking and rising into the many different parts of the earth.

First his breath became the winds and the clouds, and his voice turned into the thunders. His left eye became the sun and his right eye became the moon. His arms and legs and body grew up into the mountain ranges. His blood spilled out into the rivers. His tendons and veins stretched into the valleys, and his muscles sank down and became rich soil. His hair turned into pearls and precious stones, and his teeth and bones became gems and metals. Even his sweat and tears fell softly as the rains and sweet dews all over earth.

And so, from the body of Pan Gu, the world became very perfect.[3]

Just as the myth of Pan Gu explained the formation of the physical world, the imperial political structure can be traced to Huang Di, the legendary Yellow Emperor. The Yellow Emperor was considered the most powerful god to descend to earth. According to legend, he ruled in about the twenty-seventh century B.C. and extended the boundaries of the empire, regulated the calendar, built the first houses and cities, organized a board of historiographers, and improved commerce. And his consort is said to have invented the manufacture of silk.

Huang Di might or might not have been a real man. What is instructive, however, are the things attributed to Huang Di—the organizational achievements that allowed China to grow and prosper—for they reflect the requirements of a good emperor. That he is honored as a patron of historians is also interesting, for ancestor worship would not have been possible without detailed historical accounts of the actions and character of the dead. This illustrates the religious significance of the long tradition of Chinese history.

THE ZHOU DYNASTY

Legend has it that Huang Di also founded the Zhou dynasty (ca. 1050–256 B.C.)—the longest-lived of all Chinese dynasties—though this is certainly myth. The legend also describes the accusations of cruelty, corruption, and greed that fell upon the last emperor of the Shang, Zhou Xin. The mandate of heaven, it was said, passed to a more righteous chieftain, the leader of the Zhou, a state on the western reaches of the Shang kingdom located around the Wei River valley. King Wen, leader of the Zhou, rose against Zhou Xin and was imprisoned for his trouble. Languishing in prison, King Wen is said to have written the *I Jing* (*I Ching*), *The Book of Changes*. The trigrams (symbols made up of three lines) recorded in *The Book of Changes* were used for prophecy. King Wen's son, Wu Wang, secured his father's release and, after his father's death, vindicated King Wen with the overthrow of the Shang.

The validity of this story is unknown; much of it may be true (with the important exception of the writing of *The Book of Changes*, which was in fact written much later). The Zhou succeeded the Shang and inherited an enlarged Chinese kingdom. The Zhou claimed sovereignty over all of the northern China plains, from Beijing in the north to the Yangtze River, and from the Yellow Sea in the east to the province of Sichuan. There were independent civilizations to the south of the Yangtze that were not yet part of the greater Chinese kingdom. The western edge of the empire was the most rapidly changing. As kingdoms arose in the west, they were slowly brought into the fold of Chinese civilization.

The Zhou capital was located near the modern city of Xi'an, in Shaanxi Province, and a secondary capital flourished near the modern city of Luoyang, in Henan Province. Political control was strongest near the capitals and weakened the farther away one traveled. This empire was not yet a single political entity, but a collection of kingdoms paying tribute to the emperor as the son of heaven. Rebellion occurred frequently, and the Zhou existed by force of arms. Nevertheless, the Zhou dynasty ruled during a time when Chinese culture flowered, and the sense of what it meant to be Chinese became stronger. The family was still the principal unit of Chinese civilization, yet curiosity about the organization of the state increased. This impulse led to the richest period of philosophy in Chinese history. Literature had already been firmly established, and the Zhou added lengthy inscriptions to wondrous bronzes which had been cast for more than five centuries. Now philosophy took its place in shaping Chinese cultural life.

PHILOSOPHY AND RELIGION

This budding movement flowered during the decline of the Zhou state when tributary states rose against the emperor. "Barbarians," foreign peoples from the west and north, aided the rebelling states and China erupted into war. In 771 B.C., Chinese subjects and central-Asian horsemen armed with powerful compound bows attacked the royal stronghold near Xi'an. The Zhou king, You, was slain, but the kingdom of Zhou survived by the grace of its conquerors. King Pin, You's son, was established as ruler of the Eastern Zhou. King Pin was king in name only, and the other states were fully independent. From two historical records, the *Spring and Autumn Annals* and *The Strategies of the Warring States*, come the names for the two periods of history. The Spring and Autumn period lasted from 770 to 464 B.C. and the Warring States period from 463 to 222 B.C. Though this entire epoch is considered to be part of the Zhou dynasty, the reality is that China was in a constant state of civil war.

The civil wars eroded the old social system that was based primarily on family relationships. Forced by the rigors of war to search for useful rather than aristocratic advisors, the rulers and generals of this time opened the social order to new men. This meant opportunity for many Chinese families who were not in the highest classes. It also initiated political theories of the role of mankind and the role of government. China was in the midst of social change, and the great age of Chinese philosophy had begun.

Desiring a return to order and to traditional structures, these philosophers were conservative in outlook. Their goals were not separate from the goals of government; neither did they spurn religion, but regarded it as a natural part of an ordered life. Foremost among them was Confucius (551–479 B.C.). His family name in Chinese is Kong, and to this was attached

THE WISDOM OF CONFUCIUS

More than any other philosopher in Chinese history, Confucius shaped the practices and beliefs of Chinese society. The wisdom of Confucius survives today in *The Analects of Confucius.* The following quotations are taken from the translation by Arthur Waley:

Those who in private life behave well towards their parents and elder brothers, in public life seldom show a disposition to resist the authority of their superiors. And as for such men starting a revolution, no instance of it has ever occurred.

Clever talk and pretentious manner are seldom found in the good.

When proper respect towards the dead is shown at the End and continued after they are far away, the moral force of a people has reached its highest point.

A gentleman takes as much trouble to discover what is right as lesser men take to discover what will pay.

Behave when away from home as though you were in the presence of an important guest. Deal with the common people as though you were officiating at an important sacrifice. Do not do to others what you would not like yourself, whether it is the affairs of a State of opposition to you that you are handling or the affairs of a Family.

The gentleman is dignified, but never haughty; common people are haughty, but never dignified.

The teachings of Confucius, which were introduced during the Han dynasty, continue to influence Chinese thought. Confucius outlined the roles and obligations of individuals in relation to their families, their society, and their government.

the honorific Fuzi, meaning master; thus from Master Kong's name and title, Kong Fuzi, came the name Confucius.

Confucius's philosophy often appears remarkably practical to westerners, and so it was. He stressed the natural order of a stratified society. Obligations were clearly laid out: a child should obey his or her parents, a woman should serve her husband, a man should serve his emperor. Moreover, the rich should set an example by leading a righteous life and observing important religious ceremonies—etiquette and

THE GREAT WALL: CHINA'S HUMAN-MADE MOUNTAIN RANGE

China's geography has always provided natural borders: the Pacific to the east, the rugged mountains of Tibet to the southwest, and inhospitable deserts to the west. The northern frontier, however, stood wide open in ancient times. To make matters worse, this region of grassy steppes was the home of fierce nomadic tribesmen who would invade on horseback with frightening speed.

During the Spring and Autumn period, between the eighth and fifth centuries B.C., walled fortifications were built to protect a single village or a series of villages. But these separate walls were like mere peaks in a mountain range, easy enough to go around, and the horsemen continued their raiding. What the Chinese needed was an entire human-made mountain range to divide China from its warlike neighbors to the north.

With the unification of China by Emperor Qin Shi Huangdi in 221 B.C., the project could begin in earnest. The emperor ordered the various sections of walls to be connected into one Great Wall. Three hundred thousand soldiers and five hundred thousand peasants labored on the mammoth project, and many toiled to their deaths—their bones were thrown into the construction, making a grisly mortar. But at last, China had its northern "mountain range."

Winding over 2,000 miles between the provinces of Hebei and Gansu, the wall averages 20 to 26 feet high and 20 to 23 feet wide. Watchtowers arise every 200 to 300 yards and its top edge is marked with battlements. Yet the Great Wall never satisfied its original defensive purpose: It was breached many times. Instead, it represents the greatness of ancient China. Astronauts have reported that it is the only human-made structure visible from the moon.

ritual were all-important. At the heart of his teachings was obedience from the people to their emperor and an obligation by government to care for the people. It was a contractual relationship. As one of his many maxims states, "Do not do to others what you would not like yourself."[4]

His wisdom survives in *The Analects of Confucius*, the oldest among the Thirteen Classics. The Thirteen Classics were the kernel of the Chinese classical education. A mastery of these works was required to pass the state exams for the mandarinate—the scholar-administrators who assisted the emperor in ruling the kingdom. Confucius's teachings were continued by a number of disciples. The most famous of these philosophers is Mencius (Meng Zi; ca. 372–ca. 289 B.C.), whose work *The Book of Mencius* is also concerned with ethics and civil organization.

Confucianism was institutionalized during the Han dynasty (206 B.C.–A.D. 220) and became an integral part of Chinese civilization. Although Confucius was little concerned with religion ("keep one's distance from the gods and spirits,"[5] he warned), his teachings formed the basis of Confucianist rituals such as ancestor worship, and shrines to Confucius arose. Thus Confucianism has always been more than a philosophy in China; it is almost like a national religion, albeit an extremely pragmatic one.

The other great school of thought to emerge from the later Zhou dynasty was Daoism (Taoism), based on the teachings of the *Dao De Jing* (*Tao Te Ching*, or *The Book of the Way and Its Virtue*) of Lao Zi. The book is believed to be the collected work of many different writers, and the existence of Lao Zi (whose name simply means "the old master") is doubtful. The outlook of the Daoists is mystical. Followers sought to live in harmony with the Dao, or way, avoiding confrontation, recognition, and restraints such as government. Whereas Confucius sought to create citizens of the state, the Daoists sought an escape from state control. Both of these philosophical systems have lasted from their creation into the modern age and help shape the character of the Chinese even today.

THE QIN DYNASTY

In 221 B.C., King Zheng of Qin, a northwestern state, swept away the war and disorder of the Spring and Autumn and the Warring States periods and proclaimed himself Qin Shi

Huangdi, first emperor of the Qin (Ch'in) dynasty, after which China is named. Qin Shi Huangdi was a ruthless leader and a brilliant strategist. Through force and diplomacy, he abolished old allegiances and strengthened his hold on the empire. In the north, he connected local fortifications into the Great Wall of China, one of the wonders of the ancient world. While the Great Wall held nomadic tribesmen to the north at bay, Qin Shi Huangdi launched military expeditions into the areas that became the southern provinces of Fujian, Guangdong, and Guangxi. He also led expeditions to the west and established trade routes with the peoples of central Asia that became the Silk Road—the greatest of all ancient trading routes, connecting China with the Middle East and Europe.

The administrative structure that was established under the Qin dynasty lasted over two thousand years, until 1911. The power of the central government was strengthened over the feudal lords, and local princedoms were all but abolished. Weights, measures, currency, laws, and the calendar were standardized throughout the empire. The result was the foundation of the first Chinese political state.

Over 2,000 miles long, the Great Wall of China is one of the wonders of the ancient world. Astronauts have said it is the only human-made structure that can be seen from the moon.

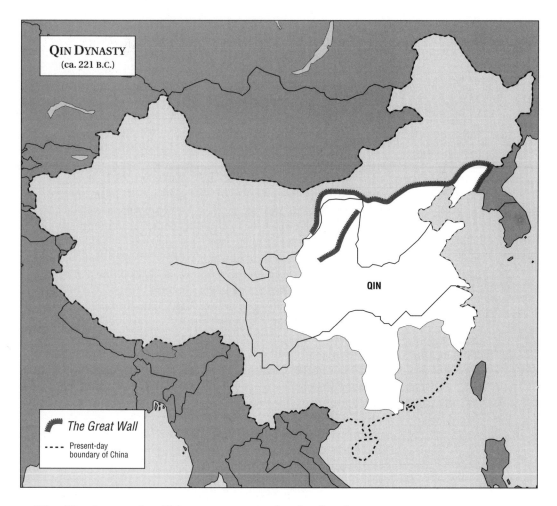

The Qin dynasty itself, however, proved to be the shortest-lived of all the Chinese dynasties; as soon as Qin Shi Huangdi died in 210 B.C., the government collapsed. His successor, the "Second Emperor," was murdered in 207 B.C. and the dynasty ended. But Qin Shi Huangdi had stamped China with his mark, permanently altering the government and expanding China's borders.

The Qin rulers had been little concerned with cultural matters. In fact, fearing rebellion from scholars, the emperor outlawed Confucianism and burned classical texts (with the exception of the imperial library) in great bonfires. Yet one of the most important of Qin Shi Huangdi's reforms was the standardization of the Chinese written language, which allowed China's culture to flourish.

THE TERRA-COTTA ARMY OF QIN SHI HUANGDI

In 1974, farmers digging a well near the ancient city of Xi'an, the seat of eleven imperial capitals, stumbled upon the tomb of the Emperor Qin Shi Huangdi. In one part of the large complex, seven thousand terra-cotta soldiers had been standing in a motionless tribute to their emperor for more than two thousand years.

The tomb complex was certainly worthy of the first emperor of the Qin dynasty, the unifier of imperial China. One ancient document, quoted in *Baedeker's China*, recorded that the tomb "is full of rare and valuable items." The document also indicated that the tomb was well guarded: "A refined system of loaded crossbows will kill anybody who approaches the grave in an attempt to rob it. The floor is shaped like a broad piece of land with rivers and lakes running through it, but instead of water they contain quicksilver." The imperial family was determined to give no tomb robber the chance to loot the sacred place.

The slow and cautious excavations that began in 1974 are still not complete. The tomb itself has never been breached, for no means has been agreed upon to protect the contents while opening it. But today, the terra-cotta army is displayed beneath a vast hall, and visitors can gaze on the foot soldiers, cavalrymen, archers, horses, and chariots. Upon close observation, it is revealed that the face of each soldier is unique, giving an eerie glimpse into the long-dead world of ancient China.

THE CHINESE LANGUAGE

Chinese is the most important of the Sino-Tibetan family of languages. It is spoken by 92 percent of the peoples of modern China (and all of the Han Chinese). Spoken Chinese has a maddening number of dialects. So different are the dialects that a person from the city of Guangzhou (Canton) cannot understand a person from Shanghai, and neither one can understand the language spoken in the modern capital of Beijing. The coastal province of Fujian has so many dialects that it is possible for two villagers living a few miles apart not to understand each other. The unifying principle of Chinese has therefore always been the written language.

Yet writing too differed. The ancient form of writing that was recorded on oracle bones was the direct ancestor of modern Chinese writing, but it was not recognizable to later Chinese. Different regions elaborated on the ancient forms in many ways until Qin Shi Huangdi established a standard imperial writing system. Because of this development, a trader on a merchant ship traveling from Shanghai to Guangzhou could present his packing lists and bills at the Guangzhou docks and all would be understood, though he could not converse about his voyage.

Chinese writing is based on characters, or symbols, called pictograms and ideograms. A pictogram is a drawing of an object, and an ideogram is a drawing that represents an idea. For example, the character for "sun" (*ri*) is a rough picture of the sun, whereas the character for "bright" (*ming*) is the combination of the pictograms for the sun and the moon—an ideogram, formed from pictograms. The ideograms often give insight into the traditional Chinese culture. The character for "peace" (*ping*), for example, is made up of a woman under a roof; in other words, a house is not harmonious without a wife or mother. And the character for "house" and "family"

Because there are so many dialects of spoken Chinese, people from different regions often have difficulty communicating. The written language, based on thousands of characters called ideograms, provides some consistency.

(*jia*), is the combination of a pig under a roof—pork is a staple of the Chinese diet and most country houses kept pigs.

There is no connection between written Chinese and pronunciation. This makes Chinese a very difficult language to learn. It requires years of memorization to master the meaning and pronunciation of the thousands of characters. And because each character is pronounced with only one syllable, the limited number of one-syllable sounds (about four hundred) caused another problem: The Chinese were running out of sounds to give their characters. To bypass this obstacle, four tones and a neutral tone were added to every word in Mandarin, the standard dialect of modern China (other dialects have varying numbers of tones). This means that a single character, when said in the four tones of varying pitch and the neutral tone—a short burst of the natural, uninflected tone of one's voice—the Chinese had increased the number of words in their language fourfold. There are around 45,000 to 50,000 Chinese characters, but modern Chinese uses only about 10,000 and the mass media only about 4,000.

Qin Shi Huangdi's language reforms gave China a greater sense of unity. Communication with the provincial governors was eased, and the role of the central bureaucracy was strengthened.

CONTACT WITH THE OUTSIDE WORLD

With the consolidation of the Chinese state came expansion. The Qin and the following Han dynasty (206 B.C.–A.D. 220) extended Chinese influences far beyond the bounds of China Proper. "China Proper" refers to the region of the eastern floodplains extending from the Great Wall southward to Guangdong Province and the South China Sea. This is the land of the ethnic Chinese—who are called the Han Chinese after the name of the Han dynasty—and the wellspring of Chinese culture.

China Proper is the agricultural center of China and is sometimes called "agricultural China." Despite the nation's vast size, food production in China has always come with great effort. Three-quarters of China Proper, the most fertile region of the country, is unable to be cultivated because of mountains, floods, lack of rain, and other factors, especially in the west and the south. All arable land in China Proper is presently under cultivation.

THE HAN DYNASTY

The expansion of the Chinese outside of China Proper allowed Chinese civilization to flourish, and a constant stream of goods and ideas reached China through contacts with other peoples. During the long reign of the Han emperor Wu Ti alone (141–87 B.C.), Chinese arms were carried westward into the province of Xinjiang, where the nomads were dealt defeats and defensive walls were erected (some of which still exist today). Korea was invaded, though not yet brought under Chinese control, and expeditions reached as far south as Tonking (Vietnam).

Contacts with the nōmads of central Asia had profound consequences for the Chinese. The western border was the great doorway to China. During peaceful times, as in the four hundred years of Han rule, a series of trade routes, known as the Silk Road, were carved through this region. The Silk Road connected a series of oases dotting the inhospitable lands of Xinjiang and central Asia. The horses and camels of the caravans teetered along this route, carrying Chinese goods as far as the Eastern Roman Empire (the Middle East) and sometimes to Rome itself.

Thus, two of the ancient world's greatest empires exchanged goods through this route for a couple hundred years, only dimly aware of each other. Chinese goods transported westward along the Silk Road included peaches, apricots, daylilies, pottery, and of course, silks. The Chinese received pearls, precious stones, glass, chives, coriander, cucumbers, figs, safflower, and sesame. The Chinese also received tribute from the central Asian tribes that had been conquered to

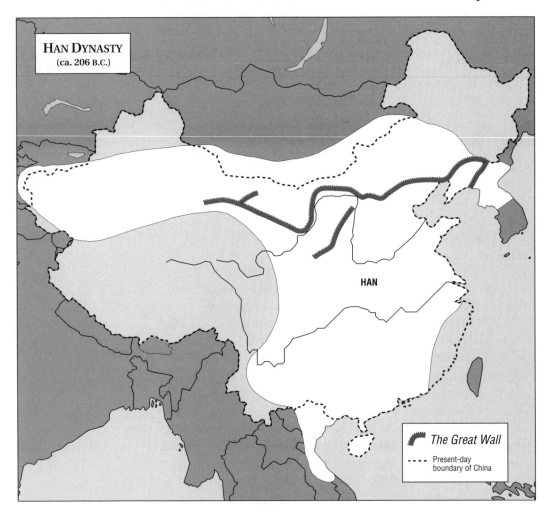

HAN DYNASTY
(ca. 206 B.C.)

HAN

The Great Wall

- - - - Present-day
boundary of China

establish the route. Along the routes there also traveled what would become the last of China's great religions: Buddhism. It crept slowly eastward at first, but by the end of the Han dynasty it was widely accepted by the Chinese.

The Chinese reinterpreted Indian Buddhism into a particularly Chinese form, reworking scriptures and founding many differing sects. Westerners, accustomed to the strict doctrines of Judeo-Christian monotheism, often find the Chinese view of religion baffling. Buddhism, like Christianity later, would be changed and blended into the Chinese pattern of life. It was not surprising to find Buddhists in China who also revered Confucius and a host of other traditional Chinese deities. For as the Christian missionaries would find out later, the Chinese have never taken an exclusive view of religion, and in no way did the coming of a new religion sweep away the old beliefs.

Under Han guidance, China prospered. The state directed improvements in the canals and water systems that advanced agriculture, and state-run factories produced bronze vessels, salt, textiles, and pottery. Intellectual pursuits also revived. The second Han emperor, Hui Di (195–188 B.C.), repealed Qin

A once-prosperous town along the Silk Road is now an archaeological treasure trove. The town, founded during the Han dynasty, includes the remains of Buddhist temples.

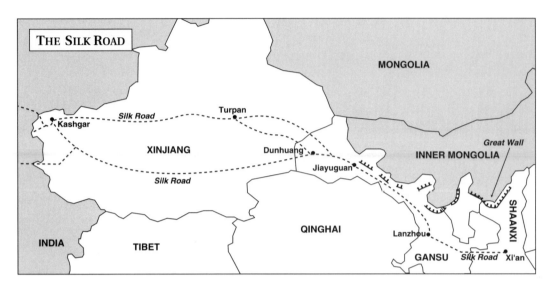

THE SILK ROAD

MONGOLIA

Silk Road

Turpan

Kashgar

XINJIANG

Dunhuang

INNER MONGOLIA

Great Wall

Silk Road

Jiayuguan

QINGHAI

Lanzhou

INDIA

TIBET

SHAANXI

GANSU   Silk Road   Xi'an

Shi Huangdi's ban on the "old books" of Confucius and other Chinese classics, and Confucianism quickly became orthodox. This new acceptance of intellectual debate allowed religious arguments to be hashed out and led to many cultural achievements. Literature and the arts revived, and history in particular received the patronage of the emperors. One work, the *Historian's Records* (ca. 90 B.C.), by Sima Qian, was of great importance, for it sought to record Chinese imperial history in its entirety.

The imperial bureaucracy of the Han was also strengthened. State exams, open to all, drew talent out of the farthest reaches of the empire. This was a prosperous time for the Chinese, and a landowning class developed. Wealth, however, was not evenly distributed and heavy taxes were levied. The court became ineffective and rebellion brewed. Finally a Daoist sect known as the Yellow Turbans, which resented royal patronage of Confucianism, toppled the empire.

The strong unity of Chinese civilization, achieved under the Qin and Han dynasties, was made evident in the following three centuries of disunity (A.D. 220–581), including the Three Kingdoms. For throughout this time of intrigues, civil war, and even invasion by various non-Chinese peoples, China remained culturally whole. Buddhism spread and great strides were made in medicine, mathematics, astronomy, botany, and chemistry. Trade also continued and new sea routes were added between China and southern Asia.

THE SUI AND TANG DYNASTIES

The Sui dynasty (A.D. 589–618), which eventually reshaped China into an empire, concerned itself primarily with strengthening its grip and completing enormous engineering projects. Sui rulers dug canals to bypass the dangerous waters of the Wei River, connecting the capital at Chang'an (near modern Xi'an) directly with the Yellow River. The government also called upon a million workers to shore up the Great Wall. The workers were often conscripted, and the imperial family was not popular with the people.

The northern "barbarians" had become a persistent threat to the Chinese and would play a great part in the future of the country. Turkic tribes from central Asia, in fact, helped establish the next dynasty, the Tang, which was partly of

THE FOUR TREASURES OF THE STUDY

Traditionally, a scholar's study was furnished with four principal articles, known as the "four treasures of the study": paper, inkstick, inkslab, and writing brush. Paper was invented in the imperial workshops sometime in the first century A.D. Cai Lun, a secretary of Emperor He Di of the Eastern Han dynasty, is credited with introducing paper to the court and improving its quality. Under his direction, paper rolled out of the imperial presses at an unprecedented rate.

Now that the Chinese had paper, they needed ink. They used an inkstick made of dried ink; it is sometimes called the Hui stick because it came from the city of Huizhou in Anhui Province. They mixed the dried ink with water on an inkslab. Because the stone for the inkslab was quarried from the Duanxi region in Guangdong, it is sometimes referred to as the Duan inkslab. Finally the brush, the traditional writing instrument of China, was used for applying the ink to paper. Chinese brushes are often quite beautiful. In fact, when laid out on a desk, the four treasures of the study make it a place of beauty even before the work begins.

The four treasures of the study are used for calligraphy (writing the Chinese characters) and for painting. Although today a Western pen is preferred for daily writing, all Chinese children are taught to write with a brush in school, and calligraphy and Chinese painting are still highly regarded arts.

Buddhism spread to China during the Han dynasty, taking on a distinctly Chinese flavor that included elements of Confucianism. Buddhist temples remain a common sight in China today.

"barbarian" descent. The Turkic horsemen and advisors helped invade Chang'an and topple the Sui, and the Tang dynasty took power. Under the second Tang emperor, Tai Tsung (ruled 627–650), China's borders were extended farther than ever before; China was for a time the largest empire on earth. Korea was once again invaded and, by 668, brought entirely under Chinese rule. In the west, Chinese armies marched through Turkistan and into Tibet and northwest India.

During the Tang dynasty, Buddhism was embraced by the court at Chang'an and devout Chinese made pilgrimages to India. The most celebrated pilgrimage was made by a monk named Xuan Zhuang. He spent sixteen years traveling around India, collecting sutras (holy texts) and learning from

Indian monks. The picaresque adventures of this Chinese monk became the basis for Wu Chengen's classic Chinese novel *Pilgrimage to the West*, in which the monk is represented as a clever monkey. The monk's adventures also entered the vast body of Chinese folktales and were celebrated in a series of Chinese operas.

Despite the allegiances between the Tang and the Turkic peoples, the Turks dealt a devastating blow to Tang armies in 751. And on the northern border a new force, the Khitan, also harassed the Tang. The empire was under siege. The Tang forged alliances with the Uighur peoples of central Asia (the areas that are now Mongolia and northern Xinjiang) to keep the other nomads from fracturing China. The Uighurs demanded heavy sums in gold and silks in return for their protection, and posed a threat themselves.

In 840 the Uighur empire collapsed after a defeat by another central Asian people, and the Tang unleashed fierce reprisals against foreigners. Uighurs in the capital were executed; followers of Nestorian Christianity, Manichaeanism, and Zoroastrianism were punished. Even the Buddhists lost favor, and many monasteries were confiscated. Pressures on the Tang finally became too great, and in 907 the dynasty collapsed.

The tribes of central Asia and the northern border of China now played a crucial role in Chinese history. Northern China, in fact, was often ruled by non-Chinese tribes. And even after the founding of the Song dynasty (960–1279), the Chinese empire controlled only China Proper, with control of the north shifting back and forth between the Khitan and the Chinese. These hostilities ceased for a time when the Song accepted a treaty by which they would pay the Khitan tribute; this was humiliating for the Chinese, who were more accustomed to receiving tribute than paying it.

The Song, though weaker than many of the dynasties before it, is remembered primarily for political and economic reforms. An advisor named Wang Anshi revised taxes so that

A portrait of a Song emperor. The Song dynasty oversaw numerous economic and military reforms.

the peasants paid less. He also arranged for loans to be made available to farmers and small merchants. Wang Anshi also reformed the navy and helped stimulate trade by sea.

With the administrative reforms of the Song came advancements in science and technology. Two earlier Chinese inventions, the compass and gunpowder, came into common use. As one China scholar put it: "All the major inventions of the pre-modern world—paper, printing, gunpowder and the compass—were known and used by the Chinese. . . . China was undoubtedly the most advanced nation in the world at this time, attaining a level which Europeans would have found hard to believe."[6] Yet not even by applying all their ingenious discoveries could the Chinese ward off the great menace that was growing in central Asia.

Ghengis Khan, a Mongol chieftain, conquered an enormous area of China in the early thirteenth century. His successors established the Yuan dynasty and eventually ruled over all of China.

THE MONGOL CONQUEST AND THE YUAN DYNASTY

In 1206, the Mongol tribes of the central Asian steppes crowned a ferocious and illiterate warrior named Genghis Khan, universal ruler of the Mongols. Civilizations in both the East and the West considered these nomadic horsemen

THE FORBIDDEN CITY

In the center of Beijing lies the Imperial Palace, a small city of brick and wood buildings topped with reddish-brown ceramic tiles. Begun by the Mongol invaders who established their capital at Beijing and founded the Yuan dynasty (1206–1368), the Imperial Palace was the residence of twenty-four emperors of the Ming (1368–1644) and Qing (1644–1911) dynasties.

The geometric regularity of the rectangular walled complex was thought to symbolize the perfect harmony of the universe. Four gates—north, south, east, and west—provide entry. The main gate, the Meridian Gate, faces south toward the bulk of China Proper and lies behind an anterior gate called the Gate of Heavenly Peace (Tiananmen). This was the traditional entryway of visiting provincial governors and other imperial officials.

Nestled within the palace are the throne and living quarters of the emperor, several libraries, gardens, kitchens, granaries, military storehouses, and numerous halls where various official ceremonies were held. The palace's nine thousand rooms also housed the imperial princes, eunuchs (servants), and the emperor's wives and concubines. (The emperor could have as many as three wives, six female favorites, and seventy-two concubines.)

Ordinary citizens were prohibited entry, giving rise to the palace's second name, the Forbidden City.

to be uncivilized, uncouth, and unworthy, and dealt with them only in trade and occasionally in battle. But the Mongols under Genghis Khan nearly smothered the light of both of these civilizations. Genghis Khan's only ambition in life was to conquer the world. "One sole sun in the sky," he said, "one sole sovereign on earth."[7] The rise of the Mongols was brilliant and swift. With a population of about one million, they conquered an area that stretched from China to eastern Europe. Undoubtedly, they considered this more or less the entire world.

Genghis still rode at the head of the Mongol hordes when they sacked and razed Beijing and slaughtered many of its inhabitants. The lands of the Song to the south proved more difficult to subdue, and Genghis died (1227) before the conquest of China was completed. The successive khans pressed forward with the invasion, while the Song resisted bravely for several decades. The Mongols, firmly established in northern China, proclaimed the Yuan dynasty (1206–1368). And in 1279, after adopting Chinese methods of warfare to conquer southern China's hills and marshes—strange land indeed for mounted raiders—Genghis Khan's grandson, Kublai Khan, overthrew the Song.

The Yuan established their capital at Khanbaliq (modern Beijing), from where the khans ruled over China and the rest of the vast Mongol empire. Although they ruled as conquerors, using foreign troops to put down rebellions and Mongol officials to govern, they slowly adopted the Chinese bureaucracy that had so effectively given Chinese civilization its continuity.

ROMANCE OF THE THREE KINGDOMS

Romance of the Three Kingdoms is a historical novel covering a period from the first year of Emperor Ling of the Han dynasty (A.D. 168) to the year A.D. 280. The novel's plot revolves around the struggle for power in the later Han dynasty and the fragmentation of China into three warring kingdoms: Wei (in northern China), Shu (in Sichuan Province), and Wu (in southeastern China).

All that is known of its author, Luo Guanzhong, comes from one of his friends and is recorded in Lai Ming's *A History of Chinese Literature*:

> Luo Guanzhong was a native of Taiyuan (in Shanxi Province), also called Wanderer among the Lakes and Seas. Although there was great disparity in our ages, he and I were good friends. But because there have been great upheavals in our time, we were seldom together. I last saw him in 1364, which was sixty-odd years ago. I do not know what happened to him.

And so one of China's greatest novelists remains a mystery to this day.

Romance of the Three Kingdoms, full of war, intrigue, and heroism, is among the most famous novels of China. The novel was so popular that its stories have formed part of the national folklore, and even people who have never read *Three Kingdoms* can recite some of its adventures.

The enormity of the Mongol empire also had its advantages. For the first time, travelers could journey in relative safety all the way from Europe to China without ever leaving Mongol lands. Muslims and Nestorian Christians traveled to Khanbaliq, and it was during the Yuan dynasty that the first Europeans saw the splendors of China (which they called Cathay). The most famous of the European travelers were the brothers Nicolo and Maffeo Polo and Nicolo's son, Marco, who traveled as ambassadors of the pope to the court of Kublai Khan. These Venetian merchants wondered at Kublai's empire and his richness. Marco served the khan from 1275 to 1292. On his return to Italy, he recorded his adventures in *The Travels of Marco Polo*.

During the Yuan dynasty, brothers Nicolo and Maffeo Polo, along with Nicolo's son, Marco, were among the first Europeans to travel to China.

Through conquest by foreigners, China had for the first time been fully opened to the world. To Europeans, Cathay was no longer a land of legend—though many Europeans, on reading Marco's account, doubted that the Chinese could be so culturally and scientifically advanced. The Yuan dynasty was not notable for developments in the arts—after all, the Mongols were just learning to read. Yet, because of this unfamiliarity with literature, drama flourished under the Yuan, and China's rich tradition of opera can be traced to this period.

THE RISE OF CHINESE NATIONALISM

The Mongols had realized Genghis Khan's dream, or nearly so. Ruling such a vast area proved to be much tougher than conquering it. As these wanderers became restless, tied to administrative duties in a foreign land, the Chinese seized the chance to evict them. In 1368, a monk named Zhu Yuanzhang and his Chinese armies captured Khanbaliq and established the Ming dynasty (1368–1644).

The Ming attempted to restore the glories of past Chinese dynasties. Their general sentiment was nationalistic. The rulers restored Confucianism and state exams, while a great imitative period of art and literature celebrated particularly Chinese themes. The government established libraries and academies, and printing flourished. One innovation was the rise of the novel. Verse had always been preferred, but the novel was more accessible to the common people, and printing made it even more so. Among the novels written during the Ming that have become classics of Chinese literature are *Romance of the Three Kingdoms* by Luo Guanzhong, *Water Margin* by Shi Naian, *Pilgrimage to the West* (celebrating the travels of the Buddhist pilgrim Xuan Zhuang) by Wu Chengen, and *Jin Ping Mei* (known in English as *The Golden Lotus*) by Xiao Xiao Sheng.

THE BIRTH OF
A NATION

China became modern in a very short time. From the end of the empire in 1911 to the founding of the People's Republic of China in 1949, China jumped from a nearly feudal agrarian state to a contender for world power with a ferociously modern outlook. But the roots of this transition lay in the Qing dynasty (1644–1911), and a long period of decline, marked by the arrival of Europeans in China, preceded China's awakening.

Early in the seventeenth century, a force had been hammered together on China's northern border by an energetic leader named Nurhaci. The Mongols to the west had declined, and Nurhaci seized the opportunity to organize the Jurched tribes of Manchuria and Mongolia into a unified body. Nurhaci organized the Jurched into military units flying various banners, and for that they are often called the bannermen (*qi ren*, in Chinese). Nurhaci, having conquered nearly all of the land north of the Great Wall, died before achieving his dream of seizing the Chinese throne. His son Abahai carried on the work and changed the name of the Jurched to the Manchus.

The Ming rulers, well aware of the menace growing to the north, were occupied with revolts within their kingdom. In the spring of 1644, Chinese rebels marched on Beijing, and the last Ming emperor, believing that the mandate of heaven had been revoked, retreated to Coal Hill on the northern side of the Forbidden City and hanged himself. The Manchus sprang into action, driving their armies southward. The Great Wall stood between them and the Chinese empire; but a wall, said Genghis Khan, is only as strong as its defenders. The defenders, in this case, were led by General Wu Sangui, who has the infamous distinction of being the man who literally opened the gates to the Manchu invaders. The Manchus established themselves in Beijing and proclaimed the Qing dynasty. China was once again under foreign rule.

In the beginning, Manchu rule was harsh. The Chinese were forced to adopt the dress and the long braided queue of the Manchus. They were forced to live in Chinese quarters of Beijing, and Manchus filled the offices of the Qing government. Slowly the Manchus adopted Chinese customs and Chinese methods of administration. Chinese mandarins were even called back to government posts (though they were forbidden to serve in their native provinces, for fear of rebellion). Chinese control once again extended east to Taiwan and west to Tibet and Xinjiang. Korea and Annam (northern Vietnam) once more became protectorates and paid tribute to the Qing. The decline of the Qing court into squabbling and decadence and the arrival of greater numbers of European ships brought about a slow decline in the second half of the Qing dynasty.

EUROPEAN SHIPS AND FOREIGN TRADE

The fortunes of European merchants and missionaries rose and fell on the whims of the Qing emperors. In 1693, Emperor Kang Xi issued an edict of toleration for Catholic missionaries, and they pressed into most of the provinces. The missionaries reached much farther inland than the merchants, while walking a narrow path between Rome's arrogant

QUEUES

To westerners who settled along the coastal treaty ports in the early twentieth century, nothing seemed so Chinese as the shaved forehead and long braid of hair worn by Chinese men. This was known as the queue. It was, in fact, not a Chinese custom at all, but a legacy of the imperial rule of the Qing dynasty (1644–1911).

After conquering China, the Manchus ordered all men to adopt the queue. Talk of the new edict spread quickly. A popular saying of the time, according to Jonathan Spence in his book *The Search for Modern China*, was: "Keep your hair and lose your head, or lose your hair and keep your head."

By the early twentieth century, the Western powers had exploited the weak Manchu government and forced opium on the Chinese population. Hatred of all foreigners, including the now effete Qing court, blazed like wildfire. Secret anti-Manchu societies arose, and talk of establishing a republic spread. To express their sentiments, members of these societies sheared off their queues. After 250 years, the queue again became a hated symbol. All of China's revolutionary leaders, including Sun Yat-sen and Mao Zedong, eventually snipped off their queues. By 1912, the Qing dynasty had been overthrown and a republic established. The queue has never again been worn in China.

assumptions about how to handle Chinese conversions and the tolerance of the Qing court. The question of what to call God in Chinese provides just such an example. The missionaries struggled with their dictionaries to find a suitable term that would satisfy Rome and not offend China's rulers. When Rome dispatched its orders on this and some other sensitive questions, the Chinese responded with violent reprisals against the Christian community.

While the missionaries fanned out into the interior, European traders remained on the coast, where they were restricted to the port cities of Guangzhou (Canton) and Macao. Portuguese ships sailing in and out of the early settlement at Macao were followed by Dutch, British, and, in 1784, American ships. The Qing treated the Europeans and Americans with contempt; they were subject to Chinese laws and restricted to foreign quarters in Guangzhou and Macao, and the Chinese were forbidden to teach the foreigners the Chinese language.

Emperor Kang Xi's 1693 edict of toleration allowed Catholic missionaries to spread throughout China.

At the same time, the European demand for tea, silks, and cottons expanded. The West was profiting from the Industrial Revolution, and in the early nineteenth century the Europeans surpassed the Chinese in technological and material wealth. This prosperity fueled a search for new markets and provided capital for trade ventures. With their newfound wealth, Europeans could afford luxury goods, and Chinese goods were prized in particular.

THE OPIUM WARS

For a time westerners paid for Chinese goods primarily in kind—by trading their goods. But because the Chinese were little interested in European goods, a trade imbalance developed rapidly. The British found a devilish solution: opium. They realized that they could trade the opium crop from British colonial India for Chinese products. By 1820, the trade imbalance had reversed: The opium trade was beginning to drain silver from China. The Qing had outlawed the importation of opium sometime earlier, but through smuggling and corrupt imperial officials, the trade thrived.

In the First Opium War, Britain attacked the Chinese in retaliation for China's attempts to stop the flow of British opium into China. The war resulted in the Treaty of Nanjing, which, among other measures, gave Britain jurisdiction over the island of Hong Kong.

The issue came to a head over the actions of one man, Commissioner Lin Zexu. Lin Zexu was an energetic official, well aware of the destruction that opium wreaked on the Chinese. In 1839, he seized opium stores, while others were handed over by the British governor-general at Guangzhou. To these Lin Zexu happily applied the torch. It appeared to the Chinese that they were acting within their rights, burning contraband in their own territory. The British saw things differently and flaunted a legalistic attitude. Trade must be free, they argued, and where there is demand for a product, the people have a right to its supply.

Gunboats shelled Guangzhou and the British crippled the Chinese navy in what became known as the First Opium War (1839–1842). Hostilities continued until the British sailed up the Yangtze, threatening communications between Beijing and the south. The Treaty of Nanjing, which officially ended the war, awarded the British the island of Hong Kong and opened five ports—Guangzhou, Amoy (Xiamen), Fuzhou, Ningpo, and Shanghai—to Western ships. In these cities, which came to be known as "treaty ports," the Europeans began to claim extraterritorial rights—that they were exempt from local laws. They started administering their own policies for their own citizens and expecting no interference from the Qing. Permanent European legations were also planted in Beijing.

The treaties did not address the question of opium, which the Europeans continued to export and the Chinese destroyed where they could. Moreover, westerners pushed for an expansion of the terms of the treaty and the Chinese attempted to restrict the concessions they had to make. The Second Opium War (1856–1858) resulted. In the south, British and French forces invaded Guangzhou, and in the north they captured the forts guarding the city of Tianjin and the road to Beijing. To prevent the capture of the capital, the Chinese capitulated. The Treaty of Tianjin set a rate for opium, resulting in legalization of the trade; opened additional treaty ports; established customs duties that favored the Europeans; and guaranteed extraterritoriality and safe conduct for Europeans. Kowloon, opposite Hong Kong, was awarded to the British and renamed the New Territories. The Americans and Russians quickly pushed for their share of the pie. As a result, the treaty ports were opened to all traders equally, and the Russians received all land north of the Amur River. To add further injury the Europeans demanded indemnities, in effect billing the Chinese for the war.

THE TAIPING AND BOXER UPRISINGS

The submission of the Qing government to foreign demands not only humiliated the Manchu court, but also undermined Qing authority in China. Laid low by opium, humiliated by unfair treaties, and subject to high taxation, the Chinese people grew discontent. Foreigners, not surprisingly, were universally resented in China, enflaming in the Chinese a spirit of nationalism. Through more than three hundred years of Qing rule, the Manchus had largely become sinicized, adopting the ways of the Chinese. But the Chinese never forgot that their masters were not Chinese, and anti-Manchu secret societies flourished.

Nowhere did these secret societies have more adherents than in the province of Guangdong. Hong Xiuquan, a fervent Christian and anti-Manchu agitator, led the most successful revolt—the Taiping Rebellion, which sought to establish a "Heavenly Kingdom." Hong claimed to be the younger brother of Jesus Christ and believed in complete egalitarianism, equality of the sexes, and strict moral conduct. By 1851, with as many as ten thousand followers, he rose in revolt with the intention of evicting the Qing and shattering a good part of China's social traditions.

The Taiping Rebellion was the first of many revolutions against Qing rule. Frederick Ward, an American adventurer who led an army opposed to the rebels, was killed in an 1862 battle (pictured).

Hong swept through southern China with surprising success. In 1853, he took the city of Nanjing, on the Yangtze River, and declared it the capital of his Heavenly Kingdom. He then marched northward, routing the disheartened imperial army. Finally, to counter Hong's army, local militias were organized and bankrolled by foreigners. This new force, known as the Ever-Victorious Army, was led first by an American adventurer named Frederick Ward, and after his death in battle, by the British general Charles Gordon (who was thereafter known as Chinese Gordon). The Ever-Victorious Army captured Nanjing in 1864. Hong committed suicide and the Heavenly Kingdom came crashing down to earth.

The Taiping Rebellion was just the first of many revolutions to come. Disastrous events now fell on China with alarming speed. Plots, conspiracies, and revolutionary societies thrived in an atmosphere of fear and excitement. The eyes of the Qing court were slowly opened to the need for modernization. The Empress Dowager Ci Xi had seized power in the court, and this clever old woman struggled with modernization and a deep hatred of foreigners. Losing a brief war with Japan over Korea showed China the effectiveness of a westernized military, for the Japanese had earlier reformed their forces along Western lines.

In the Sino-Japanese War (1894–1895), the Japanese wrested Korea from China's grip and swiftly destroyed China's northern navy. The Treaty of Shimonoseki (1895), which ended the war, awarded Taiwan to Japan and placed Japan among the powers who were carving up Chinese territory. This defeat demonstrated to the Chinese the need for reform. Ci Xi entered into the matter vigorously at first, but greed and corruption made it a slow affair.

In 1900, a new rebellion tempted the empress into folly. A band of anti-foreign warriors, known as the Righteous and Harmonious Fists—or Boxers, as the Europeans called them for their use of Chinese martial arts—began to slaughter Christian missionaries and destroy traces of Western influence in China. Churches, railways, and legations were seized and burned. The Western powers pressured Ci Xi to stop the marauders. Ci Xi made a great display of calling the imperial forces to the ready, but secretly she supported the Boxers. The chance to let the Boxers rid China of foreigners was just too tempting.

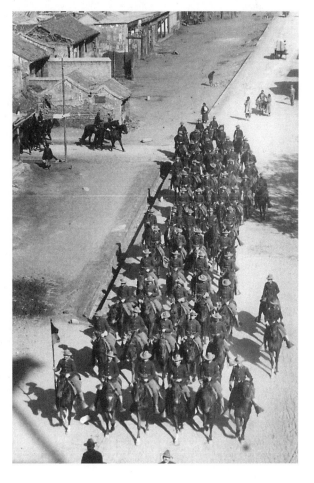

This 1901 photo shows American soldiers leaving Beijing after the Boxer Rebellion. Western forces quashed the rebellion and destroyed Beijing's Summer Palace.

The empress revealed her true feelings when the Boxers marched on Beijing, shouting their slogan, "Protect the country, destroy the foreigners." Ci Xi welcomed the rebels openly and the foreign legations were put under siege. A multinational army of European and American soldiers came to the aid of the legations on August 14, 1900, destroying the Boxers' belief that their incantations and amulets made them impervious to bullets—Western guns slaughtered them by the hundreds. Ci Xi fled the capital and the Western force looted and razed the Summer Palace, in one of the greatest acts of desecration in the history of warfare. When Ci Xi returned to Beijing, thoroughly disgraced, heavy indemnities fell upon the Qing. China was at the mercy of its conquerors.

REPUBLICAN TRIUMPH

The overthrow of the Qing dynasty was unlike any other change of power in Chinese history. When the mandate of heaven passed from the last Qing emperor, Pu Yi, the great-grandnephew of Ci Xi, it fell not on the head of a new emperor, but on the leaders of China's first republic.

The most successful republican was Sun Yat-sen, who was disgusted with the carving up of China by foreign powers and with the effete Qing. "The Chinese people," he argued, "have only family and clan solidarity; they do not have national

THE LAST EMPEROR

Pu Yi was China's last emperor. He is not remembered for anything he did, but rather as a witness to the dramatic stages of modern China's birth.

Born in 1906, Pu Yi was crowned as emperor at the age of three and lived in the Forbidden City until 1924, only dimly aware of the momentous upheavals outside the gates. He had formally abdicated the throne in 1912, at the age of six, but this was just a ceremony like many others in his highly ceremonial life. Officials of the new republican government allowed him to continue to live in the Imperial Palace. As a child he was frail, mischievous, and completely fascinated by ants. Twelve hundred gossiping eunuchs attended to his every need and flattered him obsequiously.

The arrival of a new tutor, an Oxford-educated Scot named Reginald Johnston, gave Pu Yi his first glimpse into the world outside. Pu Yi recorded in his autobiography, *From Emperor to Citizen*, that he "found the clarity of [Johnston's] blue eyes and the yellowish gray of his hair frightening" at first. But when Johnston introduced the "lord of 10,000 years" to the West, Pu Yi recalled that he discovered "intoxication with the European way of life" and found "even the smell of mothballs fragrant." He had his queue shorn off, eyeglasses ground for his myopia, and a tennis court laid out in a courtyard. And soon the sound of a foreign bell rang through the Forbidden City—Pu Yi had installed a telephone.

In 1924, Republican troops drove Pu Yi into exile, and in 1934, the Japanese set him up as the emperor of the state of Manchukuo (Manchuria). His rude treatment at the hands of the Japanese made him realize that he was nothing more than a puppet emperor. His autobiography captured his disappointment. "What sort of state is this?" he exclaimed. "Certainly it isn't the Great Qing Empire."

After the defeat of the Japanese in 1945, the Russians seized Pu Yi. He spent five years in prison in Siberia before being handed over to the communist Chinese for intensive "re-education." In 1959, Pu Yi's "rehabilitation" was complete and Mao Zedong issued a pardon for his "crimes." Upon release he became a gardener, wrote his autobiography, and even guided tours through the Forbidden City. He died in 1967, a humble citizen of the People's Republic of China.

spirit. . . . Other men are the carving knife and serving dish; we are the fish and meat."[8] Sun abandoned his life as a doctor in Hong Kong and Guangdong to struggle for the awakening of that national spirit he found lacking in the Chinese. In 1894, he formed the Revive China Society with the aim of overthrowing the Qing and establishing a Western-style democracy in China. Traveling to Japan, the United States, Britain, and other countries with overseas Chinese communities, Sun raised money for a revolution. He was undoubtedly the guiding light of the republican movement and is often referred to as the father of modern China.

After 2,000 years of dynastic rule, Sun Yat-sen, an advocate of Western-style democracy, was elected the first president of the Republic of China in 1911.

Sun was, in fact, on a fund-raising expedition when the Chinese rose against the Qing government in October 1911. Imperial troops were quickly swept aside, and by November the republicans were in power. This revolution marked the dramatic end to more than 250 years of Manchu rule and more than 2,000 years of dynastic rulership, the longest-lived political structure in history. Sun, leader of the Nationalist Party (Guomindang), was called back to China and elected the first president of the Republic of China.

The Nationalist victory was short-lived. Shortly after taking office, Sun resigned in an attempt to broker a peace with warlords in the north. The gamble failed, and from 1912 to 1949 China existed in a constant state of war. The principal players in the conflict were Sun's political descendants: Mao Zedong and Chiang Kai-shek.

Mao had been a founding member of the Chinese Communist Party (CCP) in 1921, and Chiang Kai-shek became the chief military officer in the Nationalist armies. Russian support for the Nationalist Party stifled the growth of the CCP, which served under the Guomindang flag in a coalition with the Nationalists. After Sun's death in 1925, Chiang Kai-shek inherited the leadership of the Guomindang and led the party in a conservative direction. Chiang, soon known as the Generalissimo, led a corrupt administration bankrolled by the Chinese elite, and the common people's support for the Guomindang soon began to dissipate.

In 1927, Chiang made his intentions clear. He ordered Guomindang soldiers and elements of the Shanghai underworld to slaughter union workers and Communists in

Shanghai. Zhou Enlai, Mao's political advisor, barely escaped with his life. Chiang's brutality prompted an immediate split with the CCP.

The civil war that ensued between the Communists and the Nationalists would last until 1949, interrupted only by new combatants in the field: the Japanese. In 1931, Japan seized Manchuria and began developing the rich mineral deposits to feed its war machine. This was the first step in the Japanese plan to establish an empire in Asia. Chiang dithered while the Japanese threat mounted. He hurled all of his resources into a war with the Communists, who were fighting both the Japanese and the Nationalists. Driven almost entirely out of China's cities, the CCP took to the countryside and employed guerrilla tactics. Zhu De, chief commander of the communist People's Liberation Army (PLA), summed up the strategy:

> When the enemy advances, we retreat.
> When the enemy halts and encamps, we harass them.
> When the enemy seeks to avoid battle, we attack.
> When the enemy retreats, we pursue.[9]

The tactics worked. Chiang was forced to launch a number of campaigns to stamp out communist resistance. One such campaign of 1934–1935 initiated the Long March, during which Guomindang forces pursued the PLA from Jiangxi

Province westward to Sichuan and northward to Ya-an in the province of Shaanxi—a distance of some eight thousand miles. This epic journey devastated the communist forces, but won them support from rural communities and became a centerpiece of Chinese Communist Party mythology.

THE CHRISTIAN GENERAL

After the fall of the Qing dynasty in 1911, local military chieftains, known as warlords, governed much of northern China. These were men of extraordinary character, and none more so than Marshall Feng Yuxiang, known as the Christian General.

Feng Yuxiang was a strange mix of traditional Chinese traits and Western influences. The doughy-faced general of enormous stature was born of peasant stock. While serving in the armies of Yuan Shikai—a Qing imperial commander who later succeeded Sun Yat-sen as president of China (1913–1916)—Feng converted to Christianity and became an enthusiast of Sun Yat-sen's principles. Feng's simpleness of manner was matched by his Christian zeal. "He baptized his soldiers with a hose and taught them to sing evangelical hymns and marching songs to the words 'We must not drink or smoke,'" recorded Barbara Tuchman in her book *Stilwell and the American Experience in China, 1911–45.*

"Vinegar" Joe Stilwell, who was to become the highest-ranking American officer in China during World War II, met Feng in the early 1920s. Stilwell found Feng's men learning to read and write, studying the Bible, and learning trades such as carpentry, weaving, and tailoring. Feng was bent on the moral improvement of his men. Stilwell described Feng in his diary as "a solid sort of guy with no airs who makes friends." The two plain-speaking men won each other's respect and remained friends throughout the war.

Barbara Tuchman describes the scene at Stilwell's home a few days after his death in 1946: "Mrs. Stilwell was upstairs at her home in Carmel [New York] when a visitor was announced with some confusion as 'the Christian.' Mystified, she went down to find in the hall the huge figure and cannonball head of Feng Yuxiang, who said 'I have come to mourn with you for [Stilwell], my friend.'" By 1948, Feng had turned up in the Soviet Union where he went down with a ship on the Black Sea, and the Christian General was never heard of again.

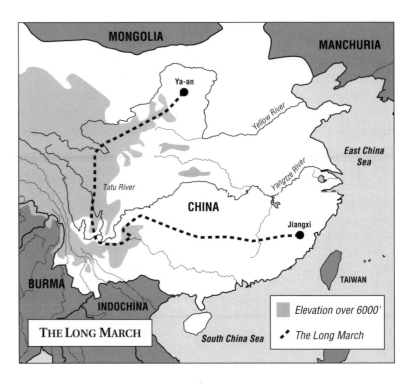

THE LONG MARCH

The Communists and Nationalists again formed a united front against the Japanese in 1936 when a warlord allied with the Communists kidnapped Chiang and forced him to sign a truce. The Japanese bombing of Pearl Harbor, Hawaii, in 1941 brought the Americans into World War II and an alliance with the Guomindang. Confident that the United States would win the war against Japan for him, Chiang concentrated his efforts on the Communists—a policy that infuriated the Americans, who were supplying the Guomindang with tons of war supplies every month by dangerous airlifts over the Himalayas.

The dropping of atomic bombs on the Japanese cities of Hiroshima and Nagasaki forced a Japanese surrender in 1945, prompting a return to full-scale civil war between the Communists and the Nationalists. From the communist base nestled in the caves at Ya-an, Mao formulated a strain of particularly Chinese communism. The power of China, he thought, lay in the countryside where most of the population lived. The Russians considered this idea unorthodox, for according to Marxist ideology, the urban proletariat must spearhead the revolution.

This peasant-based communism provided the PLA with a powerful ideology during the war. When the Communists passed through a village, they paid for their food and treated the farmers with respect. War had always been hard on Chinese villagers, and they expected to be robbed or conscripted into service. The Communists' approach provided wonderful propaganda for the PLA, and villages were soon greeting them with open arms.

The Guomindang, on the other hand, withered from corruption and inefficiency. Though Chiang had superior forces and equipment, he was disliked by the people. Hopeful Chinese flocked to the Communists, considering them their best bet for a better future. In 1949, Chiang suffered his last defeat. He led a Guomindang retreat to Taiwan and proclaimed the island the Republic of China. Mao marched into Beijing to establish China's first communist government, the People's Republic of China.

When Hiroshima and Nagasaki were devastated by atomic bombs in 1945, Japan surrendered. The end of World War II allowed the Nationalists and Communists to resume their war for control of China.

5

INTO THE WORLD OF NATIONS

The establishment of the People's Republic of China (PRC) was truly a people's victory, for the Communists had overwhelming popular support. China had been laid low by a hundred years of upheaval and the republic had been but a short-lived experiment. Addressing the people in Tiananmen Square in October 1949, Mao declared that "China has stood up."[10] The challenge now facing the victors was to build a lasting political structure on the platform of a Western ideology: Marxist-Leninist communism.

THE GOVERNMENT

The Chinese government was founded on the Russian model and is usually described as a democratic dictatorship of the proletariat, or the working class. The highest organ of state in the People's Republic of China is the National People's Congress (NPC) located in the capital of Beijing. The Congress is made up of thirty-five hundred representatives from the provinces, autonomous regions (provinces and other areas—made up mostly of non-Han Chinese—that have a small measure of political independence), municipalities, and military units. The representatives, elected for five-year terms, enact laws, formulate economic plans, and have the power to decide on foreign policy questions, including war. The president is the highest office in the NPC. Members of the standing committee of the NPC fill various other high offices. The NPC convenes annually at the Great Hall of the People in Beijing and selects the members of the standing committee.

China nominally has eight political parties: the Revolutionary Committee of the Chinese Nationalist Party, the China Democratic League, the China Democratic National Construction Association, the China Association for Promoting Democracy, the Chinese Peasants' and Workers' Democratic Party, the China Zhi Gong Dang, the September Third Society, and the Taiwan Democratic Self-Government

League. These parties, however, answer to the Chinese Communist Party, which holds a monopoly on all real political power. In fact, the National People's Congress is also controlled by the Communist Party: Candidates are almost always party members and must be approved by the party before accepting office. "The Chinese Communist Party," Mao said, "is the core of leadership of the whole Chinese people. Without this core, the cause of socialism cannot be victorious."[11]

CHINESE-SOVIET RELATIONS

Mao was proud to have taken the world's most populous nation into the fold of international communism and to have joined with the world's largest nation, the Soviet Union, in the struggle for world communism. The Soviets played an important role in the early days of the People's Republic. On December 16, 1949, Mao visited the Soviet Union, where he and the Soviet leader Joseph Stalin signed a thirty-year pact of "friendship, alliance, and mutual aid." The Soviets gave the Chinese a five-year loan of about US$300 million. In return, China reaffirmed its recognition of the Mongolian People's Republic (sometimes called Outer Mongolia, to distinguish it from Inner Mongolia, which was then, and still remains, under Chinese rule). These early acts of cooperation provided the appearance of socialist solidarity, yet a rift had existed ever since the Soviets had backed the Guomindang during the Chinese civil war, and it threatened to widen now that Mao was in the position to make policy on a national scale.

Mao was party chairman and head of state of the PRC, and he was flanked by his closest comrades from the days at Ya-an: Zhou Enlai, acting as premier and foreign minister, and Zhu De, in command of the People's Liberation Army. The unorthodoxy of Mao's peasant-based communism became apparent early on. His belief in the peasant class stemmed from two

Mao, against the advice of his Soviet allies, sought to transform China into an egalitarian society of peasant farmers.

During the Great Leap Forward, steel production initially increased due to the construction of steel mills in rural areas. Here, Mao chats with steel workers while inspecting a factory in Anhui.

sources: that China's population was overwhelmingly agrarian—Mao himself was "the rebellious son of a 'rich peasant'"[12]—and that Mao had been deeply impressed by the idyllic days at Ya-an, where the Communists had lived a truly egalitarian existence on a small scale. Mao's goal was now to transfer that model to the whole of China.

The first step was to redistribute land and transfer private property to state ownership. This was a difficult goal in a country as vast as China. The Soviets warned constantly against moving too quickly and placing too much emphasis on the peasants and the countryside. But Mao openly chastised the Soviets for their lack of revolutionary fervor: "They did not allow China to make revolution. This was in 1945, when Stalin tried to prevent the Chinese revolution by saying that we must collaborate with Chiang Kai-shek. Otherwise the Chinese nation would perish. At that time, we did not carry this into effect, and the revolution was victorious."[13]

Mao also faced opposition from within the Communist Party. Many officials agreed with the Soviets and thought that things were moving too quickly, that Mao was too radical and too unrealistic. Mao responded with a call for open criticism in 1957. "Let a hundred flowers blossom," he suggested, "and a hundred schools of thought contend."[14] And sure enough, the criticism poured forth. The "Hundred Flowers" campaign began as a debate on the role of arts and literature in a socialist society, but it quickly turned into a general criticism of Mao's leadership.

The reaction alarmed Mao, who thought that the Communist Party was betraying its original goals. As quickly as Mao had invited criticism, he unleashed a furious assault against the critics, whom he considered traditional-minded rightists. His anti-rightist campaign of 1957–1959 made the Hundred Flowers campaign look like nothing more than a trap to entice opposition into the open, where it could be swiftly crushed. This was the beginning of serious conflict within the Chinese Communist Party, and it lasted until Mao's death in 1976.

For the time, Mao had the upper hand; he was still viewed as the embodiment of the PRC by the people. And it was to the people that Mao turned for support. In 1958, he launched the Great Leap Forward, a program designed to organize the entire Chinese economy into communes, a goal that had not been accomplished in the Soviet Union even after forty years of communism. The cities and countryside bustled with activity, overseen by village activists. At first agricultural and industrial production increased, and the workers delighted in their own accomplishments.

One of Mao's goals was to even out the differences between the richer cities and the poorer countryside. City dwellers were sent to the countryside to work with the peasants, and peasants built "backyard furnaces" to aid in the production of steel. The steel output increased, but the product was of such poor quality that much of it was useless. In the end, the Leap fell short. The disruption of the Great Leap Forward caused crop failures, due to a combination of overproduction and drought, resulting in famine and economic crisis in 1960–1961.

The Great Leap Forward was condemned by the Soviet Union as folly. Russia had been moving in the opposite direction since the death of Stalin in 1953. The new Soviet premier, Nikita Khrushchev, had openly denounced Stalinism in 1956 and was moving toward détente with the West. Mao responded by accusing the Soviet leader of "revising, emasculating, and betraying" communism.[15] Relations were severed in 1960, and the dream of world solidarity within the communist bloc seemed to be at an end.

THE CULTURAL REVOLUTION

The size of the central bureaucracy that is needed to rule a country the size of China has always presented a problem for Chinese governments, from the imperial system to the communist state. Mao noticed that his own government was growing soft, and that its members had begun to live privileged, complacent lives. In 1966, he unleashed the Great Proletarian Cultural Revolution to return the country to the "Ya-an way." "To rebel is justified,"[16] announced Mao, and the country erupted with activity.

During the Cultural Revolution, students formed groups called Red Guard units and took to the streets in support of the Communist Party's cultural policies.

Students rallied eagerly to his call, forming Red Guard units. The Red Guards, dressed in their paramilitary uniforms and carrying the "Little Red Book" of Chairman Mao's sayings, unleashed terror on the country. The Red Guards smashed Western products and classical works of art, burned books they deemed to be "counterrevolutionary," and even desecrated the tomb of Confucius.

THE LITTLE RED BOOK

In 1963 Mao launched a drive to eliminate stagnation in the Communist Party bureaucracy. As a result, his sayings and slogans became popular chants throughout the country. Lin Biao, the defense minister, took the chance to publish a short book of Mao's revolutionary aphorisms under the title *Quotations from Chairman Mao*, which became known as the "Little Red Book." Lin Biao had published the book for the soldiers of the People's Liberation Army, but it quickly spread to the masses.

Mao's stature was raised to godlike heights, a phenomenon later known as "the cult of Mao." This fervor peaked during the Cultural Revolution, when millions of Mao's Red Guards swept through China armed with the Little Red Book. According to Jonathan Spence and Annping Chin in *The Chinese Century*, Liu Sola, a former Red Guard, recalled that when Mao appeared during a Red Guard rally in Tiananmen Square, in which Red Guards held high their books of quotations, "a million Red Guards wept their hearts out as if by some hormonal reaction. . . . He was divine, and the revolutionary tides of the world rose and fell at his command."

Carrying the Little Red Book and quoting from its pages became part of the ritual of Mao worship. Even Mao was surprised by the success of the book. Arthur Cotterell, in his book *China: A Cultural History*, notes that Mao, in a letter to his wife, Jiang Qing, stated that he "never imagined that my little books could have such magical powers."

Mao established the Central Cultural Revolutionary Committee to compete with the government. His aim was to re-educate the people in a socialist manner. Art, literature, and history were all to be revised on the socialist model. The old was to be entirely swept away and power returned to the radical spearheads of rural revolution. The people, however, seized the opportunity to vent any and all grievances. Humiliating public spectacles gave the Red Guards the chance to make their accusations: Students accused teachers, the poor accused the rich, the uneducated accused the educated, and country people accused city dwellers. Few Communist Party officials escaped censure. Liu Shaoqi, who had replaced Mao as head of state in 1959 (though not as party chairman, and Deng Xiaoping, one of Mao's close comrades from the Long March, were accused of being "capitalist road-ers" number one and number two. Liu Shaoqi was unconstitutionally forced from office in 1968.

Even Mao realized that chaos had engulfed China, and in August 1968 he sent the Red Guards to the countryside to work the fields. The political struggle continued, however. The head of the People's Liberation Army, Lin Biao, had had enough. Even after publishing *Quotations from Chairman Mao* (the Little Red Book), he was attacked by the Red Guards. He apparently attempted to remove Mao from power. Having failed, he escaped to Mongolia, where he was killed when his plane burst into flames.

One of the few high-ranking party officials who seemed untouchable to the Red Guards was Premier Zhou Enlai. Zhou proved to be a calming voice during the Cultural Revolution and protected many of his old comrades from the Red Guards. He undoubtedly swayed Mao toward a more moderate line. Meanwhile, Zhou worked diligently to bring China out of isolation in his capacity as foreign minister. He had cut a striking figure in 1954 at Geneva during peace talks for an end to the French war in Indochina (Vietnam). He won respect as a statesman and was greatly admired. The American secretary of state, John Foster Dulles, refused to shake his hand in Geneva, but Zhou would become instrumental in establishing relations with the United States.

CHINESE-AMERICAN RELATIONS

Mao and the Chinese Communist Party (CCP) viewed the United States as the greatest threat to China, both ideologically and militarily. After World War II, the United States continued to back Chiang Kai-shek and recognized only the Republic of China (Taiwan) as the legitimate government of China. Moreover, victory in the Pacific had established U.S. military bases in Japan and the Philippines, and soon in Korea. Mao saw this as a ring of imperialism encircling the Chinese coast.

In the 1950s the ideological battle known as the Cold War between the United States and the Soviet Union intensified. American anti-communist attitudes solidified, and the CCP became the focus of anti-communist fervor in the U.S. Congress. The Cold War flashed into actual combat during the Korean War (1950–1953). U.S. forces joined the anti-communist South Koreans against the Chinese-backed North Koreans.

Mao feared that a South Korean victory could open a door to the invasion of northern China by U.S.-backed Guomindang forces from Taiwan. Consequently, the Chinese shelled offshore Taiwanese islands. The Americans responded by positioning the U.S. Seventh Fleet between Taiwan and China and signing a defense pact with Taiwan.

The situation became alarming when the American general Douglas MacArthur, the commander-in-chief of the United Nations' forces in Korea, disobeyed orders by placing troops on the Yalu River, which separates North Korea from China, and openly advocated an expansion of the war into China. Chinese "volunteers" poured across the Yalu, driving the UN troops down the Korean peninsula. When hostilities ceased in 1953, the border between North and South Korea was re-established at the 38th parallel. Though Americans feared the rise of Red China, voices were raised against the expansion of war being advocated by MacArthur. "There is a right kind and a wrong kind of victory," argued President Truman. "The kind of victory MacArthur had in mind—a victory by the bombing of Chinese cities, victory by expanding the conflict to all China—would have been the wrong kind of victory."[17]

For the Chinese, the war was costly enough without full-scale war with the United States. They suffered nine hundred thousand casualties including Mao's eldest son, but the war gave a great boost to Chinese prestige. Although the Chinese government today has· distanced itself from the North Korean leadership, American troops still patrol the demilitarized zone along the 38th parallel. Korea is considered one of the most likely flash points for war in Asia.

One result of the Chinese participation in the Korean War was the veto of Chinese entry into the United Nations. This was something that the Americans had advocated since World War II. The Chinese seat was in fact occupied by a representative of the Republic of China (Taiwan) until 1971 when the People's Republic of China won the two-thirds majority needed to gain entry; the representative from Taiwan was then dismissed. China now has a permanent seat on the UN Security Council and plays a great role in United Nations activities.

The early 1970s proved to be a turning point in Chinese-American relations. Mao had wearied of the Cultural Revolution and authorized Zhou Enlai to negotiate with the American presidential advisor Henry Kissinger. The Americans were interested in forging a relationship after the Chinese-Soviet disagreements. Any opportunity to divide the Communists further was just good policy. The Americans also feared China's entry into the nuclear arms race. The first Chinese atomic bomb was exploded in 1964, and the Chinese were working quickly to manufacture these super-weapons. Earlier, Mao had voiced a frightening opinion of nuclear weapons. "The atomic bomb," he said, "is a paper tiger used by U.S. reactionaries to scare people. It looks terrible but in fact it isn't."[18] This provided extra motivation for the Americans to come to some agreement with the Chinese on nuclear issues.

American general Douglas MacArthur (left) wanted to expand the Korean War into China. President Harry Truman (right) opposed this policy.

PING-PONG DIPLOMACY

In 1971, in the midst of the Cultural Revolution and a widening war in Vietnam, the Chinese government invited the U.S. table tennis team to China. This surprising move resulted from secret Chinese-American talks initiated by Zhou Enlai. Zhou worked diligently to limit the worst excesses of the Cultural Revolution and, in his capacity as foreign minister, to normalize relations with the outside world.

"Chinese brilliance at table tennis," wrote Jonathan Spence and Annping Chin in *The Chinese Century*, "had in 1971 given rise to 'ping pong diplomacy' that first lifted the bamboo curtain between China and the United States." Shortly after, U.S. presidential advisor Henry Kissinger traveled to Beijing to arrange for the visit of President Richard Nixon to China in 1972. The trip proved to be a turning point in Chinese-American relations and initiated a strategic partnership to limit Soviet influence. In the course of a single trip, the world was transformed from a bipolar to a tripolar world.

President Richard Nixon's arrival in Beijing on February 21, 1972, stunned the world. The negotiations for the meeting had been held in secret and the war in Vietnam still raged. Yet Nixon, with his hard-line credentials against Communists, seemed an ideal leader to open a relationship. "The Chinese," he argued, "are a great and vital people who should not remain isolated from the international community. . . . It is certainly in our interest, and in the interest of peace and stability in Asia and the world, that we take what steps we can toward improved practical relations with Peking."[19] No concrete agreements were reached in the meeting between Mao and Nixon, but the door had been opened and China began to emerge from the isolation of the Cultural Revolution.

POST-MAO CHINA

In 1976 the deaths of Zhou Enlai and Mao Zedong initiated the second phase of the People's Republic: post-Mao China. The trial and conviction of Mao's four most fanatical supporters during the Cultural Revolution, the "Gang of Four," which included his wife Jiang Qing, settled the question of succession—moderates would succeed Mao. Further evidence was given by the fact that a number of purged officials

Deng Xiaoping, Mao's successor, favored a more moderate form of government. He enacted dramatic economic reforms, allowing private enterprise and foreign investment in China.

returned to office, most notably Deng Xiaoping, who returned as Communist Party secretary.

If there is a single person most responsible for guiding post-Mao Chinese policy, it is Deng Xiaoping. He and the moderate wing of the party characterized the Cultural Revolution as a "ten-year catastrophe." Deng was most of all a pragmatist. "It doesn't matter," he was fond of saying, "whether the cat is black or white. Its job is to catch the mouse."[20] In other words, Deng was willing to do whatever it took to move China forward, even if he upset the more conventional party officials.

Just before Zhou Enlai died, he had announced a "Four Modernizations" program for agriculture, industry, science and technology, and defense. Deng took up the banner and pushed China forward. In 1981, the first "Special Economic Zones" that allowed experimentation with private enterprise and foreign investment were established, and in the 1980s, China's huge state-run farms were broken into smaller, more competitive units in a process known as decollectivization. Deng publicly announced that foreign capital would be allowed to flow into China to stimulate the economy. He argued that "the utilization of foreign investment funds in a planned way and the promotion of a degree of individual economy are both serving the development of the socialist economy."[21]

This was radical talk for a Communist who had been with Mao since the Long March. But the results helped stave off criticism from the Communist Party, for the undeniable fact was that the Special Economic Zones were booming. The most successful was Shenzhen, across the water from Hong Kong. Shenzhen was like a tide pool collecting the runoff from the thriving Hong Kong economy, and soon it too was running over with prosperity.

Along with the newfound prosperity came luxury goods, a growing middle class, and Western influences. Deng tried to limit the Western influences, but how was he to control the forces he had set in motion? As early as 1979 a former Red Guard named Wei Jingsheng had called for a fifth modernization, democracy, to be added to the exalted four. Wei was imprisoned, but the tide was with him and the democracy movement steadily grew.

TIANANMEN SQUARE

In 1985, the Soviet leader Mikhail Gorbachev announced the policy of glasnost (open information), and by 1991 the Soviet Union was dissolved. Many thought that Chinese communism was headed in the same direction. But the question of just how far the Chinese Communist Party was willing to open up under Deng's leadership was answered at Tiananmen Square in 1989.

The death of Hu Yaobang, a much-liked reformer and party official, provided a rallying point for spontaneous protests against the CCP. The government had driven him from power for his advocacy of reform. Students from Beijing University laid wreaths at the Statue of Heroes in Tiananmen Square, in full view of the offices of the government. One billboard read: "A true man has died, false men are living."[22] The arrival from Moscow of President Gorbachev on a much anticipated visit caused the government further anxiety. The new policy of openness in the Soviet Union, ironically, had given the Chinese a chance to mend relations with the Soviets. There were many important issues to be discussed and the protesters embarrassed the Chinese government.

Finally, Deng ordered the People's Liberation Army (PLA) to clear Tiananmen Square on June 4. At first the protesters, whose numbers reached several thousand, refused to believe that the PLA would fire on them. In the end, the PLA cleared the square with tanks and live ammunition. As renowned China scholars Jonathan Spence and Annping Chin related:

> The nightmare peak of the violence in Beijing came on June 4 to 5, 1989, as many as hundreds, perhaps thousands, of Beijing residents were killed in the streets or in their homes by the random firing of the People's Liberation Army. . . . The exact number of casualties will never be known, since a news blackout was imposed on the city, hospital records were suppressed, victims' bodies were burned or removed.[23]

DAZIBAO

From the founding of the People's Republic of China to the demonstrations at Tiananmen Square, Chinese citizens have voiced their political opinions in *dazibao*, literally "big-character posters," pasted on city and village walls.

In late 1978 after Deng Xiaoping had promised greater openness in China, one Beijing wall was so littered with calls for change that it became known as the "Democracy Wall." The wall functioned much as a teahouse—a place where ideas could be aired and discussed. So brutal did the posters become by December 1978, that the government cleared the wall and banned the dazibao. Some of the critics who had been so bold to attach their names were punished. Dazibao became a symbol of resistance and in 1989 once again drew curious readers in the time leading up to the Tiananmen confrontation.

The brush, ink, and rice paper used to make dazibao are poignant reminders of the continuity of Chinese civilization. For thousands of years, dazibao were used to make public announcements in villages across China. Restrictions on press freedoms in communist China have unintentionally kept this tradition alive; should they end, the big-character posters will probably vanish from Chinese society just as broadsides did in the West.

Since the violent suppression of the revolt in Tiananmen Square in 1989, Chinese dissidents have expressed their opinions only in exile. Yet, the economic modernizations have gone forward and living standards in China have risen dramatically. The Chinese people today are harnessing their energy toward the marketplace, forced to wait for greater freedoms to follow in the wake of economic prosperity.

During the pro-democracy demonstrations in Tiananmen Square, protesters adopted Western slogans and symbols.

6

LIFE IN CONTEMPORARY CHINA

The violence at Tiananmen Square in 1989 showed the Communist Party's unwillingness to relax political control. Yet, in other arenas, Chinese society is undergoing changes that are sometimes described as a second revolution. Just as the older Chinese Communists differed from their parents who grew up under the last days of the Qing dynasty, a younger Chinese generation surprises their communist elders with their openness to Western lifestyles and values.

China is once again face-to-face with the old problem of how to modernize without losing its own cultural identity. The astounding economic progress made possible by the success of the Special Economic Zones is at the heart of many of these societal changes. New wealth has created a market for luxury goods, an increase in leisure time, and an impatience with strict government control. It has also resulted in unprecedented unemployment, growing Chinese nationalism, increased criminal activity, and more financial disparity between the cities and the countryside.

Some political scientists in the West fear that China will experience another period of disunity. But this is unlikely to happen. Despite regional differences, changing social attitudes, and lack of support for the government, the Chinese people share a strong cultural unity.

CULTURAL UNITY AND SHARED BELIEFS

One of the most striking features of Chinese life is its communal nature. The vastness of the population makes avoiding people nearly impossible. Though it has its miseries—cramped living and lack of privacy—overcrowding has been a feature of Chinese life for thousands of years. The Chinese seem content to jostle along with each other, with remarkable grace. Though the Chinese can be quite reserved with outsiders, they never stand on formality. An easygoing, friendly manner is almost a necessity in a country that houses one-fifth of the world's population, and the Chinese would consider it rude to be unfriendly even to people they consider their social inferiors.

Almost all activities are done in groups, and meals are particularly sociable. Meals are generally eaten at a round table, which makes conversation easier. Chinese food is known the world over for its refinement and subtlety. The average meal at home or in a restaurant consists of an assortment of foods served on large platters. The foods are shared among everyone at the table; ordering à la carte is strictly a foreign custom. All of the foods are usually sampled and eaten out of a rice bowl with chopsticks. A spoon is used only at the end of the meal with soup.

The Chinese people maintain a communal, friendly spirit while living in densely populated conditions.

Communal meals also play a great part in the holidays and festivals that occur throughout the year in China. These, too, are public as well as private celebrations. Two of the most important are the Chinese New Year and Moon Festival. These traditional festivals are charted by the lunar calendar. The New Year falls between the end of January and mid-February. It is a time to see family and to put things in order. A kind of spring cleaning occurs in winter. Not only are houses cleaned and decorated, but new clothes are bought and debts paid when possible. The actual celebration includes fireworks and trains of dancers costumed like dragons and lions, accompanied by clanging cymbals to ward off evil spirits. Children also receive money in lucky red envelopes from family members and local businessmen.

The Moon Festival is celebrated on the fifteenth day of the eighth lunar month and is also called the Mid-Autumn Festival. After fireworks displays, people gather to admire the full moon and children carry colorful paper lanterns. Special "moon cakes," filled with ground sesame and lotus seeds or dates, are baked for the occasion. The Chinese have celebrated these festivals for thousands of years, and they provide a sense of common heritage and continuity.

Food plays a principal role in Chinese medicine as well. In fact, food is not distinguished from medicine in China. Tea, for example, is taken as much for nourishment as for refreshment. It is always served before and after a meal to stimulate digestion. Traditional Chinese medicine relies on such natural remedies as tea, ginseng, and other plants and herbs.

THE CHINESE ZODIAC

Unlike the Western zodiac, the Chinese zodiac is based on the lunar calendar. According to tradition, the first lunar calendar was formulated by the legendary Yellow Emperor, Huang Di, in 2637 B.C.; it is still in use today. One lunar cycle equals sixty years, which in turn is divided into five twelve-year cycles. The lunar cycle that we are in today began on February 2, 1984, and will end in 2044.

A Chinese myth explains how the twelve years of the lunar cycle got their animal symbols: Lord Buddha, it was said, invited all the animals in the kingdom to see him off on a long journey. Only twelve animals showed up, and as a reward he awarded each of them one of the twelve years of the lunar cycle.

Chinese zodiac symbols are paired with the year of birth, not with the month of birth as in the Western zodiac. The Chinese still follow their horoscopes with great interest. At the beginning of each year in China, the calendar is published with horoscopes for each of the twelve symbols for the entire year. The twelve animals of the zodiac are listed below with corresponding years from 1948 to 2007.

Rat	1948	1960	1972	1984	1996
Ox	1949	1961	1973	1985	1997
Tiger	1950	1962	1974	1986	1998
Rabbit	1951	1963	1975	1987	1999
Dragon	1952	1964	1976	1988	2000
Snake	1953	1965	1977	1989	2001
Horse	1954	1966	1978	1990	2002
Sheep	1955	1967	1979	1991	2003
Monkey	1956	1968	1980	1992	2004
Rooster	1957	1969	1981	1993	2005
Dog	1958	1970	1982	1994	2006
Boar	1959	1971	1983	1995	2007

Cures are often general rather than specific. Chinese medicine is concerned with treating the whole body, and prescriptions often include lifestyle changes (a practice that is becoming more common in the West).

Western medicine is also common in China. "By 1954," one doctor explains, "the government officially recognized traditional practitioners as representing a 'medical legacy of the motherland' and thus began the dual-track process of developing Western medical practices in parallel with Chinese medical practices."[24] The quality of health care is very uneven in China today. Cities offer a choice of Western or traditional medicine (and often a combination of both), while traditional practices prevail in the countryside.

LANGUAGE AND EDUCATION

One of the greatest ambitions of the People's Republic of China, after its founding in 1949, was to remedy China's high rate of illiteracy. Attendance at school for six years became compulsory, and in 1985 it was raised to nine years. Most Chinese children today attend kindergarten and primary school. They are taught Chinese and one foreign language (usually English or Japanese), mathematics, chemistry, biology, music, art, history, and geography, and also take part in sports and other activities.

After graduation from primary school, about two-thirds enter secondary school for a period of three years. Students follow one of two courses: general education or technical training. Students who receive technical training then enter the workforce or attend a vocational college. This type of program has become increasingly popular since the 1980s, when the Chinese government began a campaign for greater scientific and technical progress. Students who pass their exams can attend one of China's many universities or colleges. This is still an enormous honor in Chinese society and only about 2 percent of the population attend universities or colleges. The Chinese have long valued education, and winning a place at a college or university ensures a high social standing. Beijing University, China's most prestigious learning institution, is as well known for the political activism of its students as for its academic excellence.

One cause of illiteracy in China is the difficulty of the language. It requires the memorization of thousands of written

FENG SHUI

For thousands of years the Chinese have practiced a form of geomancy—divination by means of geographic features—called *feng shui*. Feng shui literally translated means "wind and water." These are the two forces that shape the landscape, and the landscape is all-important in feng shui. The object of feng shui is to find or create a place of ideal harmony, where the forces of nature are given equal play and the *qi*, or energy, flows freely. To determine if the qi can flow freely, one must determine the position of mountains, rivers, hills, roads, and other topographical features.

The first known manual of feng shui was written in the ninth century A.D. by Yang Yun-sung. Since then, countless volumes have followed. After 1949, the Chinese Communists attempted to discourage the belief, along with other religions and philosophies, but it was never extinguished. Today, feng shui is widely practiced. Feng shui masters are consulted before the construction of buildings and asked to recommend the proper alignment of interior decorations and the position of furniture. Certain objects can be added to households to ward off harmful energy. The most common are the *ba gua* (eight-sided mirror) and wind chimes.

An interesting example of the use of feng shui occurred when Hong Kong reverted to Chinese rule in 1997. A feng shui master determined that Government House, the traditional seat of the British governor, was shielded from positive energy by the surrounding buildings and was collecting negative energy. The Chinese decided to move the new governor's office to a more auspicious location. Few people missed the political rebuff implicit in the feng shui master's decision.

characters and their sounds. The official language today is Putonghua, or "common speech," usually called Modern Standard Chinese, or Mandarin, in English. It is really just a standardization and simplification of Mandarin Chinese, China's most common dialect, hailing from the north. All children are required to study Putonghua at school, though at home they usually speak their regional dialect. Seven other major dialects survive: Wu, spoken in the provinces of Jiangsu and Zhejiang; Hunan, spoken in Hunan Province; Jiangxi, spoken in Jiangxi Province; Kejia, spoken by the descendants of northern Chinese who moved to Guangdong and other southern provinces centuries ago; northern Fujian dialect; southern Fujian dialect; and Yue, spoken in Guangdong and Hong Kong, which we call Cantonese.

The standardization of a national language aided in the fight against illiteracy. Two major adjustments in the teaching of Chinese aided in the adoption of Putonghua throughout the country. The first was the simplification of Chinese characters. Simplification of entire characters and of radicals (components that repeat within characters, indicating meaning or sound) had been used for centuries in script. During the republican era (1912–1949), intellectual ferment and influences from Western linguists led many Chinese to experiment with methods of simplification with the goal of increasing literacy. One such method was later adopted by the People's Republic of China (PRC), and simplified characters are taught in schools today (although Taiwan, Hong Kong, and overseas Chinese communities around the world continue to use the traditional characters).

In 1958, at the First Plenary Session of the First National People's Congress, the PRC adopted a second major innovation, called the "Scheme for the Chinese Phonetic Alphabet." The introduction of the Latin alphabet, in a form called "pinyin" served as a bridge between written and spoken Chinese. Pinyin is written beneath the characters in written text, and aids in pronunciation of the characters.

Since 1949, a comprehensive education system has been established in China in an attempt to reduce illiteracy and promote scientific and technological progress.

As pronunciation is learned, the Latin alphabet is omitted, and students read only in Chinese. Pinyin is also used for teaching Chinese to foreigners.

Putonghua received a great boost from technology. The spread of radio and television broadcasts in the standardized language has greatly increased its popularity; this trend will probably continue as more and more Chinese people buy televisions and radios. Putonghua has succeeded to some degree in bringing peoples of various dialects into greater contact with their compatriots.

LITERATURE

Just as the Chinese language has been modernized, so too has traditional Chinese literature taken a more modern course. China has a long and rich tradition of literature, but during the republican era literature became much more political. Lao She (1899–1966) and Lu Xun (1881–1936) were two leaders in this movement of socially conscious literature called the New Literature Movement.

Contemporary Chinese society drew harsh criticism from these writers. The misery of Chinese society in the 1920s and 1930s was chronicled in Lao She's *The Rickshaw Boy* and in Lu Xun's *The True Story of Ah Q*. Lu Xun compared China to an iron house, in which the Chinese were languishing:

> Imagine an iron house without windows, absolutely indestructible, with many people fast asleep inside who will soon die of suffocation. But you know that since they will die in their sleep, they will not feel the pain of death. Now, if you cry aloud to wake a few of the lighter sleepers, making those unfortunate few suffer the agony of irrevocable death, do you think you are doing them a good turn?[25]

Yet, Lu Xun did call out to wake the sleepers, and so too did his contemporaries. And the writings of Lu Xun and Lao She mark a great awakening in the history of Chinese literature.

After 1949, the leaders of the People's Republic of China not only praised literature with a social message, they required it. Mao sought "to ensure that literature and art fit well into the whole revolutionary machine as a component part."[26] "In the world today," he continued, "all culture, all literature and art belong to definite classes and are geared to definite political lines."[27] There is no doubting the power of this revolutionary literature; it played a great part in shaping the PRC. Writers who criticized their own government, however, were censored and accused of being "rightists" or "reactionaries." Even "model" writers found it difficult to walk

PINYIN ROMANIZATION

The system for the romanization of Chinese used in this book is pinyin. For the most part, pinyin is pronounced as it appears. Some of the oddities of both the pinyin system and the older Wade-Giles system are listed below.

Pinyin	Wade-Giles	Approximate English sound
b	p	b
c	ts'	ts
ch	ch'	ch
d	t	d
g	k	g
iu	iu	yo (as in *yoke*)
j	ch	j
k	k'	k
p	p'	p
q	ch'	ch
r	j	r
t	t'	t
x	hs	sh
z	ts	dz
zh	ch	j

Some familiar names of people and places are spelled out in the Wade-Giles system (still used in Taiwan). Some examples of pinyin names and terms are listed below with their Wade-Giles equivalent.

Mao Zedong	Mao Tse-tung
Zhou Enlai	Chou En-lai
Sun Zhongshan	Sun Yat-sen
Jiang Jieshi	Chiang Kai-shek
Xiang Gang	Hong Kong
taiji	tai chi
gongfu	kung fu
majiang	mah-jongg

such a narrow path. In 1966, for example, Red Guards drove Lao She to his death and many more were censored or sent to work in the countryside. Having died in 1936, Lu Xun avoided the later judgments of the PRC and was canonized by Mao. Today he is still highly respected and a museum was founded at the site of his house in Beijing.

Since the dark days of the Cultural Revolution, censorship and the struggle against it have continued. In 1986, one contemporary author, Wu Zuguang, read an article to the Chinese Writers' Association entitled "Against Those Who Wield the Scissors: A Plea for an End to Censorship." In his article, he said, "The Constitution of the People's Republic of China long ago included clauses guaranteeing freedom of speech, publication, literary and artistic creation, and other cultural activities. Interference with these freedoms is obviously a violation of the constitution."[28]

Even Deng Xiaoping argued in 1979 that "writers have the freedom to write what they want in the way they want; we should not flagrantly interfere."[29] But it was Deng who five years later unleashed the campaign against "spiritual pollution," railing against foreign and bourgeois (middle class) influences in literature. The struggle to find a public voice remains one of the defining elements on the Chinese literary scene today.

As Chinese writers struggle to find their place in the modern world, their social motivations have led to many literary innovations—notably, the political essay. At the same time, educational reforms and literacy campaigns have increased the demand for popular literature. But popular literature has been scorned by intellectuals in China for the same reason that it is so popular: because it is entertaining. Many Chinese intellectuals find the purpose of popular literature decadent and its artistic value low. Nonetheless, novels of love, adventure, and mystery are extremely popular in China, especially in the newly reclaimed territory of Hong Kong.

One of the foremost writers of the Wuxia (martial arts) genre is Jin Yong, the publisher of the Hong Kong *Mingbao* daily newspaper. Jin Yong is more concerned with history than innovation, and his novels have much more in common with classic Chinese novels, such as the picaresque *Outlaws of the Marsh* and *Romance of the Three Kingdoms*, than with the socially conscious writings of modern China. He argues, however, that there is much common ground between these two divergent forms of contemporary literature. "The leftist [socialist, political] and rightist [traditional, entertainment] views of literature," Jin Yong points out, "agree on one point: The former says one must serve the workers, peasants, and soldiers. The latter likewise says that the arts should be popularized and brought to the masses."[30]

LEISURE AND ENTERTAINMENT

Literature has in fact become more popular in China, and more people read in their leisure time than ever before. The Chinese are also fond of games. The most popular are the traditional games of Chinese chess, which is at least a thousand years old and probably much older; mah-jongg, played with tiles that resemble dominoes; and weiqi, a game of strategy played with black and white stones (weiqi is often known in other countries by its Japanese name, Go).

Parks provide space for playing games and for exercise. They are extremely important in the life of city and town dwellers. It is common to observe people playing all of these games on weekends in any of China's parks. In the early hours before work, the parks also provide space for the practice of

Parks provide space for many Chinese leisure activities, including games, exercise, and martial arts.

tai chi, an ancient form of kung fu. The elderly are especially fond of tai chi: Its slow, fluid movements increase circulation and keep the body limber. Tai chi's more bellicose ancestor, kung fu, still attracts the young and old, though modern sports have attracted many young people.

Traditionally, the Chinese viewed sports as a distraction from studying. Today, however, sports have won their place in Chinese schools. Students enjoy basketball, soccer, badminton, gymnastics, and a host of other sports. The rise in the popularity of sports in China is closely tied to the Cold War when communist countries, including China, tried to outdo capitalist countries in international competitions such as the Olympics. The Chinese displayed immense talent at these competitions in such sports as gymnastics, swimming, and fencing.

Just as the traditional games of Chinese chess, weiqi, and mah-jongg are favorite entertainments of the older generations, younger Chinese enjoy discos, karaoke, and bars. These entertainments were once frowned upon in the People's Republic of China, but today they are extremely popular in major cities and in the rapidly changing landscapes of the Special Economic Zones. The Chinese mainland is quickly coming to resemble Hong Kong, Taiwan, and Japan in this respect.

FILM

The cinema is enjoyed by both the young and old in China. Film played a powerful role in establishing the mythology of the communist PRC, and politics still permeates Chinese cinema today. "Many foreigners," writes George Stephen Semsel, who worked with the China Film Bureau, "are surprised to learn that the People's Republic of China makes almost 150 films a year (the United States made 167 feature films in 1984), and exhibits them to an audience officially numbered at 27 billion." Semsel also points out that "the Chinese have been making films since 1905, within a decade of the Lumière brothers' first films."[31]

All cinema productions in China are overseen by the China Film Bureau, which acts as a centralized production house and censorship bureau. The China Film Bureau sees the role of film as a vital part of a socialist state. It produces documentaries, propaganda, scientific and educational

Video games, karaoke, and other modern forms of entertainment have gained acceptance in Chinese cities.

movies, as well as entertainment. Historical films have always been of great interest to the China Film Bureau. A recent example was a long historical drama about the First Opium War, which resulted in Hong Kong being awarded to the British in 1842. The film was released just prior to the return of Hong Kong to Chinese administration in 1997.

In the 1980s, Chinese films began to receive attention abroad. China had emerged from the Cultural Revolution, during which time many filmmakers were sent to the fields, and now subtle, creative films began to emerge from China. This is sometimes called the Chinese "new wave," and has garnered much attention from critics and viewers outside of China. Two prominent directors who have contributed to this innovative new phase of Chinese film are Chen Kiage and Zhang Yimou, both of whom worked on *Yellow Earth* (1989). *Yellow Earth* explores the oppressive side of China's traditional values. The slow and stately camera work reflects the claustrophobic stillness of the peasants' routine lives. "What the camera invites us to look at," writes one critic, "is . . . the history of Chinese civilization, to ponder why this ancient nation and culture should lag behind others in modern times."[32]

Although the subject matter of Chinese films has been widening in recent years, *Yellow Earth* exemplifies the role of film as a meditation on society. Despite the watchful eye of the censors, films like this express an implicit criticism of a government that has not fulfilled its promises for modernization in China.

Since the 1980s, Chinese films have been shown regularly outside the country, and the international interest is having a stimulating effect on Chinese cinema. The return of Hong Kong to Chinese rule might also affect filmmaking in the PRC. Hong Kong is world renowned for its high-energy, commercial films. Hong Kong cinema is driven by entertainment value and is full of comedy, action, and the supernatural.

THE ROLE OF WOMEN

Perhaps the most remarkable change that resulted from the 1911 and 1949 revolutions was the elevation in the status of women. Traditionally, women held power only in the household and left all matters outside the house to their fathers, husbands, and even sons. Parents valued male children more than female children for two reasons: Males carried on the family name, and they could work the fields or bring honor to the family by passing state exams and entering government service. One result of this traditional prejudice was female infanticide, and the subsequent disproportionate ratio of men to women in China.

The republican governments after 1911 codified laws protecting women and expanding their rights. But the chaos of the republican period prevented women from exercising

THE RED DETACHMENT OF WOMEN

Chinese opera has been popular in China since the Yuan dynasty (1206–1368) and remains so today. In the early years of the People's Republic, the Communists enlisted the opera in their struggle for a revolutionary new society.

On his historic trip to China in 1972, President Richard Nixon attended a performance of *The Red Detachment of Women* by the Peking Opera Company, and a filmed version was shown on American television later that year. The plot is suitably revolutionary: A young woman, oppressed by a sinister landlord, flees her servitude, meets up with a hero of the Red Army, and herself joins a women's brigade, finding courage and dignity.

According to Martin Ebon in his introduction to *Five Chinese Communist Plays*, one American marveled at the ability to "combine toe slippers and rifles, and with splendid effect." As Ebon noted, "Western critics of the ballet tended to alternate between admiration of the technical side of the performances and an ironic view of its all-too-obvious political message." But it was clear that the People's Republic had succeeded in creating a vigorous new art form from the old Peking Opera.

While gender discrimination persists in the workplace, communism has allowed Chinese women to make great strides toward achieving equality.

many of these new rights. Real liberation came under the Communists. "In order to build a great socialist society," Mao wrote, "it is of the utmost importance to arouse the broad masses of women to join in productive activity. Men and women must receive equal pay for equal work in production. Genuine equality between the sexes can only be realized in the process of the socialist transformation of society as a whole."[33]

The Chinese Communist Party (CCP) guaranteed women full and equal rights. Women's organizations sprang up in cities and villages around the country, and women played a great role in local and, to a lesser degree, national communist politics. The CCP also liberated women from arranged marriages; women are now free to choose their own mates.

Women today are visible in all aspects of Chinese society. Officially they share full equality with men. It must be said, however, that discrimination against women in the workplace still exists, but it is comparable to discrimination in the West. The increasing respect for women is reflected in the more even ratio of men to women: by 1988, there were 51.1 percent males and 48.9 percent females.

POPULATION CONTROL

The current population of China has passed the 1.2 billion mark, one-fifth of the world's population. The population is heavily concentrated in China Proper. Almost the entire population of China Proper is Han Chinese. The uneven distribution of the nation's population becomes apparent with a brief glance at population density: In 1982, along the east coast, where the great cities are located, the population density was 320 persons per square kilometer, while the central provinces averaged about 71, and the thinly populated provinces of Tibet, Xinjiang, Qinghai, Gansu, and Ningxia averaged only about 10. The fertile lands of the central province of Sichuan provide an exception to this trend, showing a population density nearer to that of the coastal areas.

Although the cities of eastern China are growing rapidly, 80 percent of China's people still live in the countryside. Overpopulation is nothing new in China, and in some respects it has actually compensated for a lack of productive resources. Chinese civilization was quite literally built by teeming masses, as opposed to the West where a smaller population had to rely on invention and industry to progress. China's standard of living is increasing rapidly, yet population pressures once again threaten to keep prosperity out of reach.

Since the late 1950s, the Chinese government has enforced policies to curb growth. One such policy has been to encourage the Han Chinese to move outside of China Proper. Since the founding of the People's Republic of China in 1949, the outlying provinces, which make up more than half the area of China, have received a stream of Han Chinese, especially into Manchuria, Tibet, and Inner Mongolia. But the provinces lying outside of China Proper were not originally inhabited by Han Chinese. Today, fifty-five minorities make up the

7 percent of China's population that is not Han. These groups, for the most part, remain distinct in language and culture.

Eighteen of these minorities have populations exceeding one million: the Mongols, occupying a northern stretch of land from Manchuria all the way across Inner Mongolia; the Hui and the Uighurs in the west, distinguished by their Islamic faith; the Tibetans (whom the Chinese call the Zang); Miao; Yi; Zhuang; Boutyei; Koreans; Manchurians; Dong; Yao; Bai; Tujia; Hani; Kazakhs; Dai; and Li. The Lisu, Wa, She, Lahu, Shui, Dongxiang, Naxi, Jingpo, Kirghiz, Tu, Dahuren, Mulao, Qiang, Gelo, and Xibo minorities all have populations exceeding one hundred thousand, while the Gaoshan, Blang, Sala, Maonan, Achang, Pumi, Tajiks, Nu, Uzbeks, Russians, Ewenki, Deang, Baoan, Yugurs, Jing, Tatars, Drung, Oroqen, Hezhe, Moinba, Lhoba, and Jinao minorities have populations of less than one hundred thousand.

These minority groups play an important role in modern China. Along the southern border of China, in the provinces of Yunnan, Guangxi, Guangdong, Guizhou, and Sichuan, many native peoples have survived. Groups such as the Zhuang, Yi, Miao, Dai, and Yao live in the hills and valleys as they have for centuries. Some are closely related to the Thai

China's one-child policy has proven to be a somewhat successful—and highly controversial— means of responding to the problem of overpopulation.

and Vietnamese populations to the south. Some minority groups, the Turkish Uighurs in Xinjiang Province and the Tibetans of Xizang Province (Tibet) in particular, have aspirations to independence. These groups have grown in recent years as the Chinese government has taken more interest in preserving them and allowed some exceptions to China's strict family planning laws.

THE ONE-CHILD POLICY

The Chinese government instituted population control methods as early as the 1950s when the legal marriage age was raised to twenty-five for women and twenty-eight for men. In the early 1970s, a government population network was established that ran through all levels of the Chinese administration right down to remote villages. Through this network, the government launched campaigns to raise awareness of birth control and encourage voluntary sterilization. The government even provided free contraceptives and sterilization procedures.

These methods, which relied on the voluntary compliance of the people, fell short of their goals. Since 1979, the government has encouraged couples to limit their families to one child. This has been the most effective and most controversial of all population planning programs in China. Families who do not follow the policy can experience difficulty in finding housing and employment, and sometimes suffer from a sense of social ostracism. Families who comply and have only one child receive a "one-child certificate," which comes with financial benefits, preferential housing, and longer maternity leave.

The one-child policy has been effective in stabilizing population growth in China's urban areas, although somewhat less so in the countryside, where larger families are still prized. This policy has come under fire, however, from international human rights organizations and foreign governments, notably the United States. Stories of forced sterilizations and abortions, as well as the burden of social pressure to conform with the one-child program, have caused foreigners to look on the successful population policies with suspicion. Nevertheless, overpopulation presents China with one of its greatest problems.

EPILOGUE

THE NEXT SUPERPOWER?

China is traveling through a period of remarkable uncertainty. At the root of this lies a government pursuing two divergent paths: communist rulership and a market economy. The Special Economic Zones continue to bring a new prosperity to China, and the average living standard has improved considerably. But along with new wealth and new opportunities, China has seen the rise of individualism, so essential in an entrepreneurial economy. These developments, initiated by the government, have caused tremors of fear to ripple through the entrenched central authority. Here lies the central contradiction of Chinese society today.

Along this rumbling fault line, China travels forward, stronger than at any other time in the twentieth century. China is fiercely proud of its accomplishments and looks forward to reviving the glories of the Middle Kingdom. Hong Kong, one of the four "tiger economies" of Asia (along with South Korea, Taiwan, and Singapore), experienced tremendous economic growth in recent decades, and has been pouring investment capital and technical expertise into the Chinese economy since the 1970s. The Chinese hope that Hong Kong will stimulate further economic growth in China now that it is fully under Chinese rule.

The return of Hong Kong has allowed the Chinese to focus their energies on the island of Taiwan, the last traditional Chinese area still politically separated from the People's Republic of China. Taiwan represents a greater problem for the People's Republic. It still claims to be the only government representing all of China. Suspicion between Beijing and Taipei (the capital of Taiwan) has not lessened since 1949. What has changed more recently is the economic cooperation between Taiwan and China. Joint ventures, often organized through Hong Kong, have led to unprecedented exchanges between Taiwanese and mainland Chinese businesses. Taiwan brings to this bargain skilled personnel and

Chinese president Jiang Zemin (left) and U.S. president Bill Clinton in Beijing. In recent years, the United States has attempted to develop economic ties with China while pressuring Beijing to reform several of its domestic and foreign policies.

investment capital, while China offers a vast labor pool and cheap operating costs. The exchange has invigorated both economies and provided mainland China with much-needed guidance about the workings of a market economy.

Taiwan's independence, however, continues to irk the Chinese government. As recently as 1996, the Chinese fired rockets near Taiwan, reasserting their claims to the island. The United States—which officially recognizes only one China, the People's Republic—ordered ships from its Pacific Fleet into the Taiwan Strait, reaffirming its traditional role as the defender of Taiwan. Most Taiwanese want to rejoin the motherland, but prefer to wait until the Chinese Communist Party vanishes.

The Communist Party, however, is just as determined to play a greater part in the global economy as it is to hold on to power. China has been forging new economic links in Asia and seeking entry into the World Trade Organization. The United States has been the most vocal opponent to China's entry. In 1997, Chinese president Jiang Zemin visited the United States in an attempt to win support for China among members of the U.S. Congress and improve relations in general.

In return, President Clinton visited China in June 1998 over the strong protests of many in Congress. "There may be those here and back in America who wonder whether closer ties and deeper friendship between America and China are good," he remarked from the ancient city of Xi'an. "The answer is clearly yes. We can learn much from each other. And as two great nations, we have a special responsibility to the future of the world."[34]

That remarkable visit provided for the first time a televised exchange on human rights and the Tiananmen Square incident. For the Chinese to see their own leader defend an unpopular position on live television with a foreign dignitary was simply unheard of. The tough exchange also quieted Clinton's critics at home. "American officials were elated with the televised debate," the *New York Times* reported, "and convinced it would help justify the President's complex policy of engaging a country with fundamentally different views on freedoms."[35]

THE TRADE IMBALANCE AND HUMAN RIGHTS

Despite the success of the visit for both the Chinese and American leaders, it brought to the surface all the old grievances: the status of Taiwan and Tibet, nuclear proliferation, Chinese trade practices, and the enormous trade imbalance (China buys only about 2 percent of U.S. goods while the United States buys about 30 percent of China's goods, resulting in a $50 billion trade deficit). While there exists a rift on questions of individual freedoms, economic cooperation has been the center of Clinton's China policy, as Asia slumps into a major financial crisis. Clinton's pressure won one small victory when the Chinese agreed not to devalue their currency, which he believed would deepen the crisis in Asia.

The economy is certainly on the forefront of the Chinese agenda. In 1998, the National People's Congress elected a new prime minister—Zhu Rongji, one-time mayor of Shanghai and an outspoken reformer. Zhu has struggled for reforms for the past decade in fearless confrontations with Communist Party hard-liners. Unproductive state-run industries, corruption, and China's banking system have all drawn his criticism. His goal is to steer China away from a state-planned economy and strengthen China's financial institutions.

One telling fact about the world's reaction to the reawakening of the Chinese giant and its ambitions to play a larger part in Asia is that the officials in the United States often refer to China as the only other superpower, even though that is not yet true. (Japan still accounts for 75 percent of the economy of Asia). The People's Republic of China has all the resources to become the newest "tiger economy" of Asia. "One day, perhaps," wrote one China scholar, "it will assume the role of 'mother of all tigers.'"[36]

FACTS ABOUT CHINA

GOVERNMENT

Official name: People's Republic of China (Zhonghua Renmin Gongheguo)

Capital: Beijing

Form of government: Communist (self-described as a democratic dictatorship of the proletariat based on Marxist-Leninist Maoism)

Founding of the People's Republic of China: October 1, 1949

Official language: Mandarin Chinese (referred to as Putonghua in the PRC and as Guoyu in Taiwan, Hong Kong, and most overseas Chinese communities)

Chief administrative units:
Provinces: Anhui, Fujian, Gansu, Guangdong, Guizhou, Hainan, Hebei, Heilongjiang, Henan, Hubei, Hunan, Jiangsu, Jiangxi, Jilin, Liaoning, Qinghai, Shaanxi, Shandong, Shanxi, Sichuan, Yunnan, Zhejiang; Taiwan is considered the 23rd province but exists as an independent political state called the Republic of China (Zhonghua Minguo)

Directly administered municipalities: Beijing, Shanghai, Tianjin

Major autonomous regions: Guangxi, Nei Monggol (Inner Mongolia), Ningxia, Xinjiang, Xizang (Tibet)

PEOPLE

Total population: 1,178,400,000 (1993 estimate), making China the most populous nation on earth with one-fifth of the world's population

Population growth:
1911	374,000,000
1953	582,000,000
1978	962,000,000
1993	1,178,400,000
1995	1,203,600,000

Most populous city: Shanghai

Most populous province: Sichuan

Population density (1993): 123 persons per square kilometer

Male/female ratio (1993): 52% male, 48% female

Age breakdown (1993): 27% 15 and under, 66% between 16 and 64, 7% 65 and above

Ethnicity: Han Chinese 93%, other 7%

Literacy rate (1993): 73%, up from 10% in 1949

Compulsory education: 9 years

Birth rate per 1,000 persons (1992): 22

Death rate per 1,000 persons (1992): 7

Life expectancy at birth (1992): male, 69 years; female, 72 years

Infant mortality rate per 1,000 live births (1992): 33

State-recognized minority groups (55): Mongols, Hui, Tibetans, Uighurs, Miao, Yi, Zhuang, Boutyei, Koreans, Manchurians, Dong, Yao, Bai, Tujia, Hani, Kazakhs, Dai, Li, Lisu, Wa, She, Lahu, Shui, Dongxiang, Naxi, Jingpo, Kirghiz, Tu, Dahuren, Mulao, Qiang, Gelo, Xibo, Gaoshan, Blang, Sala, Maonan, Achang, Pumi, Tajiks, Nu, Uzbeks, Russians, Ewenki, Deang, Baoan, Yugurs, Jing, Tatars, Drung, Oroqen, Hezhe, Moinba, Lhoba, Jinao

Population breakdown by province, municipality, and autonomous region (1982 estimate):

Beijing	9,230,663	Henan	74,422,573
Tianjin	7,764,137	Hubei	47,804,118
Shanghai	11,859,700	Hunan	54,010,155
Hebei	53,005,507	Guangdong	59,299,620
Shanxi	25,291,450	Hainan	6,740,000
Nei Monggol	19,274,281	Guangxi	36,421,421
Liaoning	35,721,694	Sichuan	99,713,246
Jilin	22,560,024	Guizhou	28,552,942
Heilongjiang	32,665,512	Yunnan	32,553,699
Jiangsu	60,521,113	Xizang	1,892,224
Zhejiang	38,884,593	Shaanxi	28,904,369
Anhui	49,665,947	Gansu	19,569,191
Fujian	25,872,917	Qinghai	3,895,695
Jiangxi	33,185,471	Ningxia	3,895,576
Shandong	74,419,152	Xinjiang	13,081,538

OFFICIAL HOLIDAYS (GREGORIAN CALENDAR)

January 1	New Year's Day
March 8	International Women's Day
May 1	Labor Day
May 4	Youth Day (commemorating May 4, 1919)
June 1	Children's Day
July 1	Chinese Communist Party Founding Day (July 1, 1927)
August 1	Founding Day of the People's Liberation Army (August 1, 1927)
October 1	National Day (founding of the People's Republic of China, October 1, 1949)

TRADITIONAL FESTIVALS (LUNAR CALENDAR)

Spring Festival (Chinese New Year): celebrated for at least 3 days between the end of January and mid-February (the most important of all Chinese festivals, comparable to Christmas in the West)

Lantern Festival: 15th day of the 1st lunar month

Dragon Boat Festival: 5th day of the 5th lunar month (around the end of May)

Moon Festival (Mid-Autumn Celebration): 15th day of the 8th lunar month

Festival of the Ancestors: early April; also known as the Day of Purity and Light

LAND

Area: 3,716,154 square miles (9,627,343 square kilometers)

Greatest east-west distance: 2,725 miles (4,400 kilometers)

Greatest north-south distance: 2,500 miles (4,100 kilometers)

Location: China lies roughly between latitudes 18 and 54 degrees north, and between longitudes 71 and 135 degrees east

Bordering countries: Korea, Russia, Mongolia, Kazakhstan, Kyrgyzstan, Tajikistan, Afghanistan, Pakistan, India, Nepal, Bhutan, Myanmar (Burma), Laos, Vietnam

Bordering bodies of water: Yellow Sea, East China Sea, South China Sea

Highest mountain range: Himalayas, average elevation 20,000 feet (6,100 meters)

Longest river: Yangtze (Chang Jiang), 3,720 miles (6,000 kilometers)

Largest lake: Qinghai Lake, 1,600 square miles (4,160 square kilometers)

CLIMATE

Climatic zones:
    Tropical monsoon climate (southern China)
    Subtropical climate (southern China)
    Cold winter climate ("Yellow" northern China)
    High continental climate (Manchuria)
    Upland climate (Tibet)
    Dry climate (northwestern China)

Average temperatures of selected cities:
    Harbin (northeastern China):
        January, -4°F (-20°C); July, 73°F (23°C)
    Beijing ("Yellow" northern China):
        January, 23°F(-5°C); July, 77°F (25°C)
    Lanzhou (central China): January, 8°F (-13.3°C); July, 73°F (23°C)
    Ürümqi (northwestern China):
        January, -4°F (-20°C); July, 68°F (20°C)
    Lhasa (Tibet): January, 28°F (-2.2°C); July, 59°F (15°C)
    Hong Kong (south coast): January, 59°F (15°C); July, 81°F (27°C)
    Shanghai (east coast): January, 41°F (5°C); July, 81°F (27°C)

ECONOMY

Official currency: renminbi (RMB); principal units of renminbi in descending order of value are the yuan, mao (or jiao), and fen (1 yuan = 10 mao; 1 mao = 10 fen). There are banknotes of 1, 2, 5, 10, 50, and 100 yuan and mao; and coins and banknotes for 1, 2, and 5 fen. In June 1998 $1 equaled 8.27 yuan RMB, and 1 yuan RMB equaled $0.12.

Major industries: iron and steel, textiles, agricultural implements, trucks

Major crops: grain, rice, cotton, tea

Labor force: 60% in agriculture, 25% in industry and commerce

Composition of national income:

Sector	1952	1978	1987
Industry	19.5%	49.4%	45.7%
Agriculture	57.7%	32.8%	33.8%
Commerce	14.9%	9.8%	10.1%
Construction	3.6%	4.1%	6.6%
Transportation	4.2%	3.9%	3.7%

Gross national product (GNP) (1989): $393 billion

Per capita GNP (1989): $360

Imports (1992): $76.3 billion; partners: Hong Kong, 20%; Japan, 20%; United States, 11%

Exports (1992): $80.5 billion; partners: Hong Kong, 38%; Japan, 16%; United States, 7%

Television sets: 1 per 8 persons

Radios: 1 per 9.1 persons

Telephones: 1 per 89 persons

Daily newspaper circulation (1989): 37 per 1,000 persons

NOTES

INTRODUCTION: THE MIDDLE KINGDOM

1. Quoted in *The Oxford Dictionary of Quotations*. New York: Oxford University Press, 1980, p. 359.

CHAPTER 1: THE LAND

2. Quoted in *Baedeker's China*. New York: Macmillan Travel, 1996, p. 19.

CHAPTER 2: THE EXPANSION OF THE CHINESE POPULATION

3. Yuan Ke, *Dragons and Dynasties: An Introduction to Chinese Mythology*. Translated by Kim Echlin and Nie Zhixiong. New York: Penguin, 1993, pp. 1–3.

4. Confucius, *The Analects of Confucius*. Translated by Arthur Waley. New York: Vintage, 1983, p. 162.

5. Quoted in Stephen G. Haw, *A Traveller's History of China*. New York: Interlink Books, 1997, p. 63.

CHAPTER 3: CONTACT WITH THE OUTSIDE WORLD

6. Haw, *A Traveller's History of China*, pp. 116–17.

7. Quoted in Haw, *A Traveller's History of China*, p. 121.

CHAPTER 4: THE BIRTH OF A NATION

8. Quoted in John Bartlett, *Familiar Quotations: A Collection of Passages, Phrases, and Proverbs Traced to Their Sources in Ancient and Modern Literature*. 16th edition. Boston: Little, Brown, 1992, p. 601.

9. Quoted in James E. Sheridan, *China in Disintegration: The Republican Era in Chinese History, 1912–1949*. New York: The Free Press, 1975, p. 247.

CHAPTER 5: INTO THE WORLD OF NATIONS

10. Quoted in Bartlett, *Familiar Quotations*, p. 436.

11. Mao Zedong (Tsetung), *Quotations from Chairman Mao Tsetung*. Beijing: Foreign Languages Press, 1972, p. 2.

12. Arthur Cotterell, *China: A Cultural History*. New York: Mentor, 1990, p. 319.

13. Quoted in Cotterell, *China: A Cultural History*, p. 290.

14. Mao, *Quotations from Chairman Mao*, pp. 302–303.

15. Quoted in Cotterell, *China: A Cultural History*, p. 303.

16. Quoted in Jonathan D. Spence and Annping Chin, *The Chinese Century: A Photographic History of the Last Hundred Years*. New York: Random House, 1996, p. 196.

17. Quoted in Bartlett, *Familiar Quotations*, p. 655.

18. Quoted in Cotterell, *China: A Cultural History*, p. 295.

19. Quoted in Bartlett, *Familiar Quotations*, p. 733.

20. Quoted in *Baedeker's China*, p. 75.

21. Quoted in Cotterell, *China: A Cultural History*, p. 325.

22. Quoted in Cotterell, *China: A Cultural History*, p. 326.

23. Spence and Chin, *The Chinese Century*, p. 240.

CHAPTER 6: LIFE IN CONTEMPORARY CHINA

24. Tom Williams, *Chinese Medicine: Acupuncture, Herbal Remedies, Nutrition, Qigong, and Meditation for Total Health*. Rockport, MA: Element, 1995, p. 3.

25. Quoted in Helmut Martin, *Modern Chinese Writers: Self-Portrayals*. Armonk, NY: M. E. Sharpe, 1992, p. 276.

26. Mao, *Quotations from Chairman Mao*, p. 301.

27. Mao, *Quotations from Chairman Mao*, p. 299.

28. Quoted in Martin, *Modern Chinese Writers*, p. 39.

29. Quoted in Martin, *Modern Chinese Writers*, p. 37.

30. Quoted in Martin, *Modern Chinese Writers*, pp. 172–73.

31. George Stephen Semsel, ed., *Chinese Film: The State of the Art in the People's Republic*. New York: Praeger, 1987, p. 1.

32. Ma Ning, quoted in Semsel, *Chinese Film*, p. 82.

33. Mao, *Quotations from Chairman Mao*, p. 297.

Epilogue: The Next Superpower?

34. Quoted in "Clinton Starts Visit to China by Answering Critics in U.S.," *New York Times*, June 26, 1998, p. A1.

35. Erik Eckholm, "Surprising Exchange on Rights on Chinese Television," *New York Times*, June 28, 1998, p. A1.

36. Willem van Kemenade, *China, Hong Kong, Taiwan, Inc.* New York: Knopf, 1997, p. x.

CHRONOLOGY

B.C.

ca. 600,000
Homo erectus, early humans, in China

ca. 80,000
Homo sapiens, modern humans, in China

ca. 2650
Reign of the Yellow Emperor, Huang Di (legendary)

ca. 2100
Founding of the Xia dynasty (legendary); Chinese Bronze
Age begins

ca. 1600
Founding of the Shang dynasty

841
Earliest certain date in recorded Chinese history

770
Beginning of the Spring and Autumn period

ca. 650
Iron casting begins

551
Birth of Confucius

479
Death of Confucius

463
Beginning of the Warring States period

221
Qin Shi Huangdi establishes the Qin dynasty

214
Qin Shi Huangdi's Great Wall project is completed

206
Founding of the Han dynasty

ca. 90
Sima Qian finishes the first complete history of China

A.D.
ca. 65
Buddhism reaches China

105
Cai Lun introduces paper to the royal court

184
The Yellow Turbans rebel

220
End of the Han dynasty; beginning of the Three Kingdoms

ca. 250
Tea drinking begins to spread through China

589
Founding of the Sui dynasty

605
Completion of the Grand Canal, linking the Yangtze with the Yellow River

618
Founding of the Tang dynasty

ca. 629–645
Xuan Zhuang's pilgrimage to India, the subject of Wu Chengen's *Pilgrimage to the West*

668
Chinese armies conquer Korea

868
Earliest surviving dated printed book produced in China

ca. 901
Paper money first used in China

907
End of the Tang dynasty

919
Chinese begin to use gunpowder

960
Founding of the Song dynasty

1194
The Yellow River overruns its banks and changes course

1206
Founding of the Yuan (Mongol) dynasty

1275–1292
Marco Polo in China

1279
The Yuan (Mongol) dynasty completes the conquest of China

1368
Founding of the Ming dynasty

1421
The Ming move their capital to Beijing

1514
Portuguese ships reach China

1535
Portuguese establish a trading colony at Macao

1592
Japanese invade Korea

1598
Chinese evict the Japanese from Korea by force of arms

ca. 1640
The first tea is brought to Europe

1644
Founding of the Qing (Manchu) dynasty

1720
Tibet is incorporated into the Chinese empire

1729
Opium is outlawed by imperial edict

1793–1794
The British arrive in China

1839–1842
First Opium War

1842
Treaty of Nanjing awards Hong Kong Island to the British, and Shanghai becomes a "treaty port"

1851–1864
Taiping Rebellion

1855
The Yellow River overruns its banks and changes course; the northern section of the Grand Canal is rendered useless

1856–1858
Second Opium War

1858
Treaty of Tianjin opens additional treaty ports to the north

1860
British and French forces enter Beijing and destroy the Yuan Ming Yuan summer palace

ca. 1862
Empress Dowager Ci Xi seizes power at the Qing court

1894–1895
Sino-Japanese War

1895
Treaty of Shimonoseki ends war with Japan and awards Taiwan to the Japanese

1898–1900
Boxer Uprising

1900
Siege of the foreign legations in Beijing; Western troops occupy Beijing

1904–1905
Russo-Japanese War; Japan takes over Russian holdings in Manchuria

1908
Empress Dowager Ci Xi dies; Pu Yi, the last emperor, takes the throne

1911
Qing dynasty overthrown

1912
Founding of the Republic of China

1914
World War I begins; Japan seizes German concessions
in China

1917
China enters World War I against Germany

1919
May 4th Movement: Chinese students protest against the
Versailles settlement

1921
Chinese Communist Party is founded in Beijing

1925
Sun Yat-sen dies; Chiang Kai-shek becomes leader of the
Nationalists

1931
Japan invades Manchuria

1933
The League of Nations condemns Japan's aggression
against China; Japan walks out of the League

1934
Pu Yi becomes puppet emperor of the Japanese state of
Manchukuo (Manchuria)

1934–1935
Communists undertake the Long March as they flee from
the pursuing Nationalists

1936
The Xi'an Incident; the Chinese Nationalists and Communists form a united front against Japan

1937
Outbreak of war between China and Japan

1945
The USSR attacks the Japanese in Manchuria; the United States drops atomic bombs on Hiroshima and Nagasaki; Japan surrenders

1949
Proclamation by the Communists of the founding of the People's Republic of China; the Nationalists under Chiang Kai-shek withdraw to Taiwan and proclaim the island the Republic of China

1950
U.S. Seventh Fleet sent to the Taiwan Strait to prevent a communist invasion of the island; China sends troops into Korea

1951
The People's Liberation Army invades Tibet

1953
Korean War ends

1957
"Hundred Flowers" campaign

1958
The Great Leap Forward; People's Communes established

1960
Split between China and the Soviet Union

1962
China defeats India in a war over the border of Tibet

1964
China explodes its first atomic bomb

1966
Start of the Great Proletarian Cultural Revolution

1971
Death of Lin Biao; the People's Republic replaces Taiwan at the United Nations

1972
President Nixon visits China

1975
Zhou Enlai announces the "Four Modernizations" program

1976
Deaths of Zhou Enlai and Mao Zedong

1977
The "Gang of Four" are arrested

1979
The United States recognizes the People's Republic of China

1981
First "Special Economic Zones" established

1988
Hainan Island becomes a province

1989
Suppression of the pro-democracy movement at
Tiananmen Square in Beijing

1993
Exchange rate of the Chinese yuan allowed to float

1997
Deng Xiaoping dies; President Jiang Zemin visits the
United States; former British colony of Hong Kong reverts
to Chinese rule

1998
President Bill Clinton visits China

CHRONOLOGY OF CHINESE DYNASTIES

B.C.

ca. 21st–16th centuries: Xia dynasty (legendary)

16th–11th centuries: Shang dynasty

ca. 1050–771: Western Zhou dynasty

770–256: Eastern Zhou dynasty

770–464: Spring and Autumn period

463–222: Warring States period

221–206: Qin dynasty

206 B.C.–A.D. 220: Han dynasty

A.D.

220–280: The Three Kingdoms

265–420: Jin dynasty

304–439: The Sixteen Kingdoms (northern China)

420–589: The Northern and Southern dynasties

589–618: Sui dynasty

618–907: Tang dynasty

907–960: The Five dynasties

960–1279: Song dynasty

1206–1368: Yuan (Mongol) dynasty

1368–1644: Ming dynasty

1644–1911: Qing (Manchu) dynasty

Suggestions for Further Reading

Aisin-Gioro Pu Yi, *From Emperor to Citizen.* New York: Oxford University Press, 1988. The last Manchu emperor describes his life of privilege as part of his "rehabilitation" under the Communists. Invaluable firsthand account of the last days of the Qing dynasty.

Associated Press Writers and Photographers, *China: From the Long March to Tiananmen Square.* New York: Henry Holt, 1990. A photographic history of modern China.

Wolfgang Bartke, *Who's Who in the People's Republic of China.* Armonk, NY: M. E. Sharpe, 1987. Biographical entries of leading Chinese citizens.

David Bonavia, *The Chinese.* New York: Lippincott & Crowell, 1980. A general, journalistic account of the Chinese.

Confucius, *The Analects of Confucius.* Translated by Arthur Waley. New York: Vintage, 1983. The writings of China's greatest philosopher.

John Fraser, *The Chinese: A Portrait of a People.* New York: Summit Books, 1980. A study of contemporary Chinese society by a former correspondent for the *Toronto Globe and Mail.*

Roger Garside, *Coming Alive: China After Mao.* New York: McGraw-Hill, 1981. Garside's stated purpose is to "tell the story of how life returned to a nation that had been half-dead."

Liang Heng and Judith Shapiro, *Son of the Revolution.* New York: Vintage Books, 1984. A firsthand account of the Cultural Revolution.

Reginald F. Johnston, *Twilight in the Forbidden City*. New York: Oxford University Press, 1985. The Oxford professor's memoirs of his years as tutor to Pu Yi, the last emperor of the Qing dynasty.

Eduardo del Rio (Rius), *Mao for Beginners*. New York: Pantheon Books, 1980. An entertaining and informative summary of Mao's life and his beliefs by the left-leaning Mexican journalist Rius.

Edward H. Schafer and the Editors of Time-Life Books, *Great Ages of Man: Ancient China*. New York: Time-Life Books, 1967. An illustrated introduction to the high points of ancient Chinese civilization.

Orville Schell, *To Get Rich Is Glorious: China in the Eighties*. New York: Pantheon Books, 1984. Schell recounts his impressions of a visit to China in 1983–1984 and observes a rapidly changing society.

Sterling Seagrave, *The Soong Dynasty*. New York: Harper & Row, 1986. A lively, gossipy portrait of nationalist China's most powerful family and their connections with the United States.

Edgar Snow, *Red Star over China*, revised and enlarged edition. London: Allen & Unwin, 1963. A description of early days of Chinese communism and life in Ya-an written by an American journalist.

Jonathan D. Spence and Annping Chin, *The Chinese Century: A Photographic History of the Last Hundred Years*. New York: Random House, 1996. An oversized volume of photographs from about 1900 to the Tiananmen incident.

Cao Xueqin, *The Story of the Stone (The Dream of the Red Chamber)*, 5 vols. New York: Penguin, 1973–1986. China's most famous classical novel.

Sun Zi (Sun Tzu), *The Art of War*. New York: Delacorte Press, 1983. The most famous Chinese book of military strategy by a fifth-century B.C. general.

WORKS CONSULTED

BOOKS

Baedeker's China. New York: Macmillan Travel, 1996. A detailed travel guide to the People's Republic of China, including essays on China's topography, economy, history, and arts and culture.

John Bartlett, *Familiar Quotations: A Collection of Passages, Phrases, and Proverbs Traced to their Sources in Ancient and Modern Literature.* 16th edition. Boston: Little, Brown, 1992. An indispensable guide to who said what, focusing primarily on popular quotations in Western society.

The Cambridge History of China. New York: Cambridge University Press, 1978– . Probably the definitive history of China in the English language. Volumes on modern China are yet to be completed.

Arthur Cotterell, *China: A Cultural History.* New York: Mentor, 1990. An engaging overview of Chinese history from the beginning to the People's Republic.

Martin Ebon, *Five Chinese Communist Plays.* New York: John Day, 1975. Five early communist plays that helped shape the mythology of communist China, edited and with an introduction by Martin Ebon.

John King Fairbank, *The United States and China.* Cambridge, MA: Harvard University Press, 1979 (fourth edition). A scholarly introduction to modern China and Chinese-American relations.

Stephen G. Haw, *A Traveller's History of China.* New York: Interlink Books, 1997. A well-written, concise overview of modern China.

Charles Hucker, *China's Imperial Past.* Stanford, CA: Stanford University Press, 1975. An insightful summary of China from the beginning to the early part of the twentieth century.

Yuan Ke, *Dragons and Dynasties: An Introduction to Chinese Mythology*. Translated by Kim Echlin and Nie Zhixiong. New York: Penguin, 1993. An explanation of old Chinese cosmology and a retelling of myths and folktales from China.

Willem van Kemenade, *China, Hong Kong, Taiwan, Inc.* New York: Knopf, 1997. A study of the interplay among three distinct Chinese economies.

Owen and Eleanor Lattimore, *China: A Short History*. New York: W. W. Norton, 1975. A quick introduction to China by world-renowned China scholars. This book is particularly good on World War II, which the authors saw firsthand in China.

Colin Mackerras and Amanda Yorke, *The Cambridge Handbook of Contemporary China*. Cambridge, U.K.: Cambridge University Press, 1991. A statistical overview of modern China, complete with graphs, charts, time lines, and biographical sketches of notable Chinese.

Helmut Martin, *Modern Chinese Writers: Self-Portrayals*. Armonk, NY: M. E. Sharpe, 1992. A collection of essays by modern Chinese writers on their craft and the state of literature in late-twentieth-century China. It includes short biographical essays of each author and a lucid introduction by Martin.

The Oxford Dictionary of Quotations. New York: Oxford University Press, 1980. A reference work of notable quotations from around the world; entries include author and source.

George Stephen Semsel, ed., *Chinese Film: The State of the Art in the People's Republic*. New York: Praeger, 1987. A collection of essays on the origins and themes of Chinese cinema after 1949, including a detailed introduction to China's film industry by Semsel.

James E. Sheridan, *China in Disintegration: The Republican Era in Chinese History, 1912–1949*. New York: The Free Press, 1975. Sheridan tackles the political awakening of post-imperial China and traces the intrigues and battles between the Nationalists and Communists.

Jonathan D. Spence, *The Search for Modern China.* New York: W. W. Norton, 1990. An in-depth study of the forces that shaped modern China, from the Ming dynasty to the protests at Tiananmen Square. Jonathan Spence is undoubtedly the most famous living China scholar writing in English.

Jonathan D. Spence, *To Change China: Western Advisers in China, 1620–1960.* New York: Penguin, 1980. Spence traces three hundred years of Chinese-American relations through Western visitors to China.

Barbara W. Tuchman, *Stilwell and the American Experience in China, 1911–45.* New York: Bantam, 1972. A fascinating portrait of "Vinegar" Joe Stilwell, the highest-ranking U.S. general in China during World War II, and a history of American relations with the nationalist Chinese government.

Tom Williams, *Chinese Medicine: Acupuncture, Herbal Remedies, Nutrition, Qigong, and Meditation for Total Health.* Rockport, MA: Element, 1995. An enthusiastic explanation of the theories behind Chinese medicine and of some specific Chinese medical practices, written for westerners who are unfamiliar with Chinese medicine. This book does not include an explanation of the efficacy of Chinese medical practices in Western medical terms.

Robert L. Worden, Andrea Matles Savada, and Ronald E. Dolan, eds., *China: A Country Study.* Washington, DC: Federal Research Division, Library of Congress, 1988. A detailed study of China's people and geography with charts and statistics.

Mao Zedong (Tse-tung), *Quotations from Chairman Mao Tse-tung.* Beijing: Foreign Languages Press, 1972. The "great helmsman" speaks for himself in what became known as the "Little Red Book."

Jianying Zha, *China Pop: How Soap Operas, Tabloids, and Bestsellers Are Transforming a Culture.* New York: The New Press, 1995. A study of the rapid transition in contemporary Chinese culture.

PERIODICALS

"Clinton Starts Visit to China by Answering Critics in U.S.,"
New York Times, June 26, 1998.

Erik Eckholm, "Surprising Exchange on Rights on Chinese
Television," *New York Times*, June 28, 1998.

INDEX

PICTURE CREDITS

ABOUT THE AUTHOR

Robert Green holds a B.A. in English literature from Boston University and is currently working toward his M.A. in journalism at New York University. He is the author of thirteen other books, including biographies of Alexander the Great, Tutankhamen, Julius Caesar, Hannibal, Herod the Great, and Cleopatra, as well as biographies of six British monarchs and *Vive La France: The French Resistance During World War II*. He lives in New York City where he has been studying Chinese for the past two years.